Library Technology Planning for Today and Tomorrow

LIBRARY INFORMATION TECHNOLOGY ASSOCIATION (LITA) GUIDES

Marta Mestrovic Deyrup, Ph.D.
Acquisitions Editor, Library Information and Technology Association, a division of the American Library Association

The Library Information Technology Association (LITA) Guides provide information and guidance on topics related to cutting-edge technology for library and IT specialists.

Written by top professionals in the field of technology, the guides are sought after by librarians wishing to learn a new skill or to become current in today's best practices.

Each book in the series has been overseen editorially since conception by LITA and reviewed by LITA members with special expertise in the specialty area of the book.

Established in 1966, LITA is the division of the American Library Association (ALA) that provides its members and the library and information science community as a whole with a forum for discussion, an environment for learning, and a program for actions on the design, development, and implementation of automated and technological systems in the library and information science field.

Approximately 25 LITA Guides were published by Neal-Schuman and ALA between 2007 and 2015. Rowman & Littlefield took over publication of the series beginning in late 2015. Books in the series published by Rowman & Littlefield are:

Digitizing Flat Media: Principles and Practices
The Librarian's Introduction to Programming Languages
Library Service Design: A LITA Guide to Holistic Assessment, Insight, and Improvement
Data Visualization: A Guide to Visual Storytelling for Librarians
Mobile Technologies in Libraries: A LITA Guide
Innovative LibGuides Applications
Integrating LibGuides into Library Websites
Protecting Patron Privacy: A LITA Guide
The LITA Leadership Guide: The Librarian as Entrepreneur, Leader, and Technologist
Using Social Media to Build Library Communities: A LITA Guide
Managing Library Technology: A LITA Guide
The LITA Guide to No- or Low-Cost Technology Tools for Libraries
Big Data Shocks: An Introduction to Big Data for Librarians and Information Professionals
The Savvy Academic Librarian's Guide to Technological Innovation: Moving Beyond the Wow Factor
The LITA Guide to Augmented Reality in Libraries
Digital Curation Projects Made Easy: A Step-By-Step Guide for Libraries, Archives, and Museums
Library Technology Planning for Today and Tomorrow: A LITA Guide

Library Technology Planning for Today and Tomorrow

A LITA Guide

Diana Silveira

ROWMAN & LITTLEFIELD
Lanham • Boulder • New York • London

Published by Rowman & Littlefield
An imprint of The Rowman & Littlefield Publishing Group, Inc.
4501 Forbes Boulevard, Suite 200, Lanham, Maryland 20706
www.rowman.com

Unit A, Whitacre Mews, 26-34 Stannary Street, London SE11 4AB

British Library Cataloguing in Publication Information Available

Library of Congress Cataloging-in-Publication Data Available

ISBN 978-1-5381-0931-1 (hardback : alk. paper) | ISBN 978-1-5381-0932-8 (pbk. : alk. paper) | ISBN 978-1-5381-0933-5 (ebook)

♾ ™ The paper used in this publication meets the minimum requirements of American National Standard for Information Sciences Permanence of Paper for Printed Library Materials, ANSI/NISO Z39.48-1992.

Printed in the United States of America

To my family, friends, and colleagues who have supported me
throughout my career.

Contents

List of Figures

Preface

The prospect of technology planning can seem overwhelming and time consuming, especially for those who work in an already short-staffed library. If this is your situation, you may be thinking,

- We haven't had a technology plan up to now, and things seem fine. Why change?
- There's not enough money to add new equipment, so why should we even bother with planning for technology?
- Let's just continue to deal with technical issues as they arise.
- It's easier to "go with the flow" and buy new technology when we have some extra funds.
- The city's (or county's or school district's) information technology department handles technology for our library, so we don't need to worry about it.

Such thinking will prevent your library from becoming all that it could be. In truth, creating and implementing a technology plan can help you open the door to the modern era. Sound planning can lead to increased funding for technology in your library. Most important, a solid technology plan can help you create an environment that truly meets the needs of the community your library serves.

Lofty goals? Maybe so, but this is 100 percent true. Having a plan will allow you to prepare for the future instead of merely reacting to technology crises. Determining the technological needs of the library and its users will equip you to better allocate existing funds.

Library Technology Planning for Today and Tomorrow was created to help those who work in libraries—especially those who are new to the planning process. The objective of this book is to guide library staffs in working through the entire process of creating a customized technology plan. This LITA Guide will also show library staffs the importance of technology planning; it demonstrates how the process of creating and implementing a plan can help the library, its staff members and users, and the community as a whole. Designed to break down the planning process into manageable steps, it provides a practical and useful guide for the first-time planner. As readers work through each step in the process, they move closer to completing a plan that addresses the needs of their library and their community.

This LITA Guide was developed with knowledge I've gained in more than fifteen years of working in libraries and with libraries as a trainer and consultant. As a former public librarian, I've also worked with academic, school, and special libraries while on the staff of a multitype library consortium and as a consultant. As a library consultant, I have helped libraries of different types to use technology effectively.

My planning philosophy is simple: Planning should be a practical process that makes it easier to achieve your goals. Time is short and library funding is tight; both time and money must be applied reasonably if your library is to be successful. As consultant, I've gained an outsider's perspective of the process of developing and successfully implementing technology plans. From this I've identified the key areas on which a library must focus for success. This book's practical nature, with each step clearly laid out, equips the time-crunched librarian to work logically through a planning process that will help the library accomplish its objectives.

UNITY LIBRARY SYSTEM

Throughout this book, the Unity Library System is used extensively as an example to illustrate issues and to bring concepts to life. These examples bring the theoretical to a more practical level where the reader can readily understand each issue and how it can be resolved. As a library system, Unity does not actually exist; rather, it is a composite of many libraries I've worked with and of my imagination.

The Unity Library System was created to bring real-world examples into the planning process. For the purposes of this book, it is a library system located in a rural county and consisting of two locations: Beach Library and City Library. The area around Beach Library is predominantly rural with a more senior population; however, the demographics of this area are beginning to change and are becoming increasingly urban as the county focuses on economic development in the immediate area of Beach Library. City Library is in a suburban area and is within walking distance of a high school. In recent years, both libraries have suffered from decreased funding and from an overall lack of focus on technology. As a result, both fell behind in providing either adequate technology tools for their staffs or appropriate technology resources for their communities.

Recently, the Unity Library System gained a dynamic new director who, along with the library staff, began to plan how they could reenergize the community about the library. Modernizing the library's technology is a significant component of that plan. The Unity staff recognized a need to upgrade the library's current technology offerings. They also wanted to introduce some of the cutting-edge technologies that are bringing renewed interest and buzz to libraries across the nation.

Throughout this book, scenarios attributed to the Unity Library System will be explored to illustrate opportunities—as well as missteps—to help you understand each concept.

GETTING STARTED

Library Technology Planning for Today and Tomorrow demonstrates the cascading effect that technology issues can have throughout the library and shows how planning can help alleviate many issues before they are problems. In addition, this LITA Guide looks at the long reaches of technology planning and the ways a good plan can help reenergize your library, meet the needs of your community, and even exceed your library's goals.

Following a logical order, this book takes you through the process of first developing and creating a written technology plan and then carrying out that plan through implementation and evaluation. The book's unique focus on meeting the needs of your community through technology planning provides a practical manual for library staffs to create and achieve goals that meet their specific user needs. By helping library managers to first step back and look at the big picture and then to delve into the details, *Library Technology Planning for Today and Tomorrow* addresses three main questions:

1. What are the goals for your library?
2. How can you utilize technology that the library already has, and what additional technologies are needed to meet the library's overall goals and to carry out its mission?
3. How do you successfully implement these technologies?

As a library consultant, I've found that a library without a technology plan often lacks the foundational tools necessary to create such a plan. I have assisted small- and medium-sized libraries with the technology planning process, taking them from the very first steps through implementation of new hardware, software, and other technologies. I have also conducted training for libraries on the entire planning process with detailed focus on specific aspects of planning. Often this process had to start at the most basic step: identifying what the library has. This may seem like a trivial point, but many libraries only "sort of" or "mostly" know what hardware and software they have; they have no true inventory system.

By beginning with a technology audit or assessment, library staffs are able to see the larger picture as they begin to understand the fundamental gaps existing in their technology resources. Thus, in chapter 1, we start with the basics of conducting a technology audit to understand what your library has and what it may lack. In chapter 2, we move into helping you understand the technology options for your library through trendcasting and analysis of current issues such as security, as well as for developing a plan to conduct a comprehensive community assessment. Chapter 3 focuses on assessing the data you've collected as you move to analyzing statistics and then to looking both inward at the library and outward at the community to consider the library's overall mission in serving its constituents. This information is essential in determining the library's technology needs.

Once needs have been identified, the next step is to create concrete goals and outcomes that become the focus of your technology plan. These goals tie specific technology enhancements and expansions to specific community needs; they provide a plan for purchasing technologies that best fit your library's needs as well as details to use in persuading funders of those needs. For example, simply declaring "We need a 3-D printer" as a single, unsupported statement is unlikely to influence decision makers positively. On the other hand, relating the acquisition of a 3-D printer to a larger community-based initiative that fosters small businesses can help justify the need and will likely have a more positive outcome.

In addition to laying out goals and outcomes, chapter 4 moves into a practical mode of helping you select the technology that will work best in your library, decide how to place and implement technologies to greatest advantage, and—most importantly—learn to create a budget.

By following this book's outline, you will stay focused on technology planning from beginning to end. Once the background work has been done and a rough plan has been developed, chapters 5 and 6 show you how to turn the data collected into a workable plan with a realistic implementation schedule. Going further, the book will guide you through the project management phase of bringing the technology plan to life, including the critical aspects of marketing to staffs and users and communicating regarding these new and exciting changes. Chapter 7 helps you create a plan for training both staffs and users on the new technologies—not only in the implementation stage but also as an ongoing process that is especially necessary to keep staff comfortable and knowledgeable with all the technology offered by the library.

Just as it includes plans for training, a successful technology plan must also address the regular maintenance of technology. Chapter 8 explains why this is important and how a maintenance schedule should be structured.

Chapter 9 shows you how to use the planning process to answer these key questions: Are you meeting your goals? Are the outcomes what you expected? Are the results positive or negative? If the results are negative, can you address the issue and transform a failure into a success? Finally, chapter 10 discusses how to use the plan you create today as a foundation for future planning, and chapter 11 explains how to move forward with your plan.

Let's get started on your technology plan! I hope you find this LITA Guide as practical and easy to work through as it is intended.

Acknowledgment

Thank you to Faye Roberts, who expertly and patiently assisted me with editing this book.

Chapter One

Conducting a Technology Assessment

The first step in creating a technology plan for your library is to conduct an assessment of existing technology. It is vital to know what you already have before considering future plans or what to purchase.

In simplest terms, performing a technology assessment or audit means counting and listing all forms of technology currently in your library. It's not sufficient to look at a few selected areas. Look at all the hardware and software throughout the entire library system. To make the audit truly beneficial, though, you need more than just a list. The assessment should not only identify computers; it should look at the whole picture of the library's current technology. This picture—a snapshot of existing resources— will help you create a document you can use for triage of your library's needs, a guide for filling any gaps. A full technology assessment will also include statistics on your technology usage and on the availability of that technology.

Developing a technology plan, or even just purchasing technology without an assessment, can lead to several issues, including the following:

- Replacing technology that is not the highest priority or skipping technology that is in dire need of replacement.
- Buying technology that the library may already have. As you will discover in your assessment, your library has a lot of technology. Some is probably tucked away in departments or branches and not included on your main inventory lists. For example, perhaps the Friends of the Library purchased several iPads for your literacy department. These may or may not be on the main inventory list and might not be known to the information technology (IT) staff or to those in other departments or locations who may need them. When it comes to determining needs, if you know what's on hand you may find there is existing equipment to fill those needs.

- Missing the big picture. By conducting a technology assessment, you will gain an understanding of what your library has currently and how this is utilized by the public and by staff. Moving forward, the assessment will let you identify unmet needs and plan for changes and additions in technology so you can better serve your users.
- Failing to create buy-in for new technologies. Libraries frequently need to justify funding and must seek outside funding to update technology. The unsupported statement "We need new computers" does not hold weight with funders. However, a statement such as the following can positively influence decision makers: "Our small business computers are being utilized 95 percent of the hours the library is open. Last month alone more than 230 users focused on learning new job skills, utilizing small business resources, and managing their businesses. Unfortunately, these machines are currently running an out-of-date operating system and users are learning old software. These computers will need to be replaced by the end of the year."

CURRENT TECHNOLOGY: A SNAPSHOT IN TIME

The technology assessment will capture a complete picture of your library's current setup. If you're developing your first comprehensive inventory, you're likely to discover there's a lot more technology in your library than you thought. So that you don't overlook anything, let's explore the different types of technology that should be included.

There are four main areas of technology to evaluate.

- Internet access
- Routers and firewall(s)
- Hardware (staff and public)
- Software (staff and public)

Internet Access

Internet access is your library's core technology. Most other technologies, whether based within the library or brought in by users, rely on Internet access. From computers to wireless printers, to users' smartphones and many maker resources, the Internet is used heavily throughout the library. Adequate bandwidth is critical to serving your users. Without proper bandwidth, technologies will not function properly; both staff members and users will have a substandard experience.

Your technology audit should include confirmation of the current bandwidth along with current upload and download speeds. It's important to confirm the speeds for computers in a variety of different configurations.

These can include but are not limited to computers in different parts of the library or in each branch as well as hardwired technologies and technologies connected via Wi-Fi that are used in different parts of the building. As part of your service contract with your Internet Service Provider (ISP), you are guaranteed specific speeds; ensure you are receiving them.

How can you verify the speed of your Internet? Several online tools will help test your speed. I prefer the open-source tool Measurement Lab. Measurement Lab is not an Internet provider but a research-based organization formed by supporting partners that include New America's Open Technology Institute, Google Open Source Research, and Princeton University's PlanetLab (M-Lab n.d.). To use Measurement Lab, go to https://www.measurementlab.net and navigate to Tests. Select the performance test, NDT (Network Diagnostic Tool).

Routers and Firewalls

Routers and firewalls are hardware and software that control and monitor networks. Routers and firewalls manage your network using specific rules configured by library staff. These rules include, but are not limited to, the following:

- Creating multiple networks with varying levels of access and permissions
- Setting permissions for ranges of Internet Protocol (IP) addresses that are allowed or not allowed to enter your network
- Creating a line of defense that prevents unauthorized access to staff and user devices

Routers and firewalls protect your library and your users; therefore, these need to be kept up to date by reviewing the settings and updating software regularly. Review settings for routers and firewalls to ensure they meet the needs of your library staff and users. In addition, take the time to document your settings if this has not already been done. Router and firewall settings are among the types of sensitive information most frequently restricted to just one staff member—and issues of access can arise if that staff member leaves. All this information should be stored in an accessible location for multiple, authorized staff members to access when needed.

Hardware

Hardware includes all electronic equipment and apparatus available for use within the library by the staff and the public. While computers are obvious examples of hardware, other types of equipment to capture during your assessment include printers, barcode scanners, copiers (staff and public), servers, and any small, portable devices such as tablets and e-readers. Your technology assessment should document all in-house and circulating technologies. Peripherals such as mice, styluses, adaptive devices, and other key components of your technology should be inventoried as well. While this might seem a small matter, you need to capture every bit of technology so it can be considered as you plan for future updates and replacement of the technology it supports.

It's equally important to maintain and update technology used in makerspaces as well as any equipment used during specific time periods or designated for specific library programs; these should be included in your technology assessment too. Examples of these might be 3-D printers and robotics as well as engineering and coding resources such as Bloxels, SnapCircuits, Makey Makeys, Spheros, and Ozobots. Be sure to include projectors, fax machines, and scanners. Finally, do not leave out departmental mobile phones or digital cameras.

Often specialized hardware that was purchased through separate funding sources, rather than through the traditional purchasing route, is missing from a centralized inventory maintained by the IT staff. For example, a 3-D printer that was purchased for the children's department or a new makerspace paid for with funds from a grant, Friends of the Library group, or other local organization may not have been added to the library's property records. Devices such as these need to be included in the assessment to complete the full picture of your library's technology.

Software

It is vital to inventory and understand the software your library currently has installed on both staff and public computers. The inventory should include purchased software and any free software that the library maintains on its computers; both types require investments of staff time and expertise. Consider including additional fields on your inventory spreadsheet to reflect licensing and account management details. These fields may include the log-in information for access, a license number, or a reference to an overall license agreement. For example, if your library subscribes to the Adobe Suite and has access to five licenses, you will need to ensure those five are utilized in ways that best fit the library's needs. In addition, tracking specialized software, such as that used by finance, human resources, technology services, or other departments, will help ensure timely license renewals. It will also ensure that other issues with updates and maintenance do not fall through the cracks.

CREATING YOUR ASSESSMENT

A spreadsheet is the easiest way to create an understandable picture of the technology identified in your assessment. Spreadsheets make the data much more manageable, allowing it to be more easily filtered, sorted, and otherwise manipulated. For libraries with a large enough budget, several inventory management systems are available to explore. However, this book focuses on low-cost solutions and a spreadsheet as an inexpensive, but highly effective, way to manage your technology.

You can download a ready-to-use technology assessment template at goo.gl/TFL8PN. This template, a data collection form, is a spreadsheet with columns labeled for frequently used fields. The document includes separate worksheets for hardware and software; these have been prepopulated with sample data. The template can be downloaded or copied for use as the basis of your library's technology assessment.

The fields needed for hardware and software will vary, so it's easier to inventory these separately. I recommend either including two worksheets in your spreadsheet or creating two separate files: one for hardware and one for software. Your hardware spreadsheet should include most of the following information for each type of technology:

- Name. This is the name by which the library staff refers to the unit, for example, Reference Desk Staff Computer 1.
- ID number. This field can designate the device's internal property control number assigned by your library, city, school, or institution.
- Serial number. This number is vital for warranty and troubleshooting issues. Having the manufacturer's serial number or barcode recorded in this document will save staff time and effort. Serial numbers are often attached to the back or bottom of devices. However, with smaller devices like Ozobots, podcast microphones, or computer mice, serial numbers are often found only on the original packaging or order form; if the numbers were not recorded at the time of purchase, you may not have access to them.
- Item description. A brief description quickly identifies the device, for example, "Acer—All-in-One Public PC with Windows 8."
- Network name. For any device in the library to be connected to the Internet, it must first be connected to a local network. Each local network will have a unique name such as "Downtown Branch—Staff," "Free Public Wi-Fi," or something similar. Each network will have been created with different access and usage rules. It is important to understand what devices are connected to the Internet through the library's networks and to which local network each device is assigned. Chapter 4 explains the value of

having different local networks within your library to optimize bandwidth and to keep library data and users' information secure.

- IP address. Each device within your library that is connected to your network or to the Internet has a unique Internet Protocol address, a numeric label assigned to the device. The IP address is needed to secure devices and to connect them to databases seamlessly. IP addresses also help identify individual technologies within your network.
- Location. Identify the device's primary physical location, such as the branch or overall department of the library.
- Department. If the library has multiple locations, a second location field specifying the department is needed to clarify a device's location. To keep equipment records straight, it is vital to identify both branch and department. For example, the library will likely have several of the same PC models, bar code scanners, and other core devices all located in different departments within the same building. In addition, technology can migrate over time. For instance, a laptop purchased for adult services may be utilized later in the teen department. This inventory can help determine where devices actually live within the library.
- Public/staff usage. This simple field designates who can use a device. Adding this field allows you to use the spreadsheet's filter to quickly identify what technologies are available to whom.
- Condition. Does the technology need to be replaced? Are there maintenance issues? Knowing the condition of current technology is especially important, so adding this information to the assessment will be invaluable in determining technology gaps and needs.
- Vendor. Having the vendor's name and maintenance contact information stored in the assessment document brings all the vital information about your technology into one place.
- Years of service left. It's important to understand how long your current technology might last before it needs to be replaced. The service period can vary depending on your library's policies and budget. Some libraries consider the end of the warranty period to be the end of life; others may use a guideline such as replacing computers every certain number of years to ensure that efficient, modern devices are available for all staff members and users.
- Version. Note the current version of software installed on each device and whether a newer version of the software is available. For example, in 2017, some machines were still running the Windows 8 operating software even though Windows 10 was the current, standard version.

The final assessment document should be a practical and useful tool for your library. If specific, suggested columns are not useful to you, they can be deleted. Add any other columns that may be of use within your library. Additional columns to consider include the following:

- Responsible party. Who on the staff (either a person or a position title) is charged with maintaining a device? Knowing this will help identify holes in your current maintenance plan. Without a responsible party, any technology is at risk of having technical issues and even breaking. For example, at City Library, we realized that the 3-D printer had no responsible party assigned. While staff could help users and were able to operate the machine, no individual was charged with running software and firmware updates or with providing overall preventive maintenance to the machine. As a result, the 3-D printer lacked updates and was in need of routine maintenance. In the long term, missing updates and maintenance will cause the 3-D printer to develop issues with bad prints and filament clogging. The end result will be less uptime and frustrated staff members and users.
- Critical level. Is this item of technology critical or noncritical to the day-to-day operations of the library? While the goal is to have all the technology working all the time, it's especially important to identify those items most crucial to the library's mission. For example, having the reference department printer out of service can cause far more disruption to services than does a malfunctioning staff printer in the administration office. Both printers are important, but triaging your technology will help ensure that you and your staff know where to focus resources.

A more extensive sample audit showing a wide variety of hardware is available at https://goo.gl/2nBVSv. The sheet used to collect software information should include many of the same fields as above. In addition, include the following:

- Login information. How do you access the administrative page for the software? This is the page used for payment, statistics, and support.
- Licensing. This field should include basic licensing information such as number of seats, a license number, or a reference to an overall license agreement.
- License renewal. This is the date by when the software needs to be renewed.

Sample Audit

Looking at our Unity Library System, we will now explore a small portion of technology within the Beach Library's adult services department. Adult services at Beach Library includes not only reference but also genealogy, public

PCs, lending laptops, the makerspace, and staff technology. For example, if we are looking at just the genealogy area, the following equipment might be listed:

Genealogy—Dell desktop computer
Genealogy—wired keyboard
Genealogy—wired mouse

For each aspect of this genealogy computer, we captured the ID number, description, network (where applicable), IP address, location (branch), usage, condition, vendor, and years of service remaining. On the software side, we also recorded that the Dell desktop computer located in the genealogy department is set up for access to Ancestry.com (using one of the library system's three licenses), has Microsoft Office, and is running Windows 10. Recording all of the data about the machine at once saves time later because there's no need to keep revisiting the computer for additional information.

Logistics of Collecting Data

Whether you're responsible for a multibranch system or for only a single branch, the idea of a full technology assessment can seem daunting. You can't carry out this process without laying eyes on each item in each department of the library. Luckily, there are resources to help you streamline the job.

First, if possible, create a team to help you gather the needed data. Explaining the purpose and the reasoning behind the audit will help lower staff barriers to this task. When staff members understand that having more data about the current technology will help facilitate new and more regularly scheduled technology updates and purchases, they will become excited about the process of assessment.

An interactive online form will simplify the process of data collection. The following tips will help make your form more effective.

- Standardize vocabulary. Wherever possible, indicate options by creating drop-down menus or radio buttons. Listing choices such as public/staff, years remaining, or vendor options from drop-down menus will help keep answers consistent and will mean less data to clean up afterward. A standardized or controlled vocabulary enables easier filtering, sorting, and other manipulation of data during evaluation too.
- Provide examples. Examples or guidelines for each answer will help staff members think beyond the basic technology within their area. For example, a prompt asking about makerspace or lending-library technologies may help the staff remember to list Ozobots or 3-D printers.

An online form with all relevant fields makes data entry easier for staff members who are located in different locations, floors, or departments. Those in each department can add their inventory manually. Beach Library Branch, for example, consists of eight main departments: children's services, adult services, administration, technical services, literacy, circulation, information technology (IT), and genealogy. While the IT staff was in charge of creating the overall audit document, other departments were charged with entering their own technology.

There are several software options for creating online survey forms. The survey requirements for a technology audit are minimal, so I recommend using either software already utilized within your library or a free or "freemium" program (commercial survey software that offers a light version at no cost). One free surveying tool is Google Forms (https://docs.google.com/forms). An example of a Google Form used to collect data is located at https://goo.gl/tKajiJ.

Keeping the Assessment on Track

Oversight will be needed to make sure that the assessment is comprehensive and that it is completed on time. Here are some best practices to help the process run smoothly.

- Create deadlines. There should be a firm deadline for entering data and for reviewing entries. It is also vital to have library managers who are committed to your charge and supportive of deadlines to keep the assessment at the top of staff priorities.
- Expect surprises. While preparing the assessment, you are likely to discover aspects of technology that have been overlooked in your current IT maintenance plan. For example, at the Beach Library a computer used by volunteers was not listed on the IT staff's inventory. This computer, while connected to the main network, was not receiving updates. Unmaintained technology like this can be a vulnerability affecting the library's entire network. Out-of-date browsers, out-of-date security, and other software requiring updates can expose a computer to a range of security issues that can and will take down your entire network. For example, in 2017, a bug in the older versions of the Microsoft XP operating system was used in a massive cyberattack that affected multiple businesses and libraries throughout the world; computers with updated operating systems were not affected.
- Create reminders. Staff members have many responsibilities and may be multitasking multiple projects. Taking inventory may not be their top priority—but the assessment is a necessary and vital step, especially for a

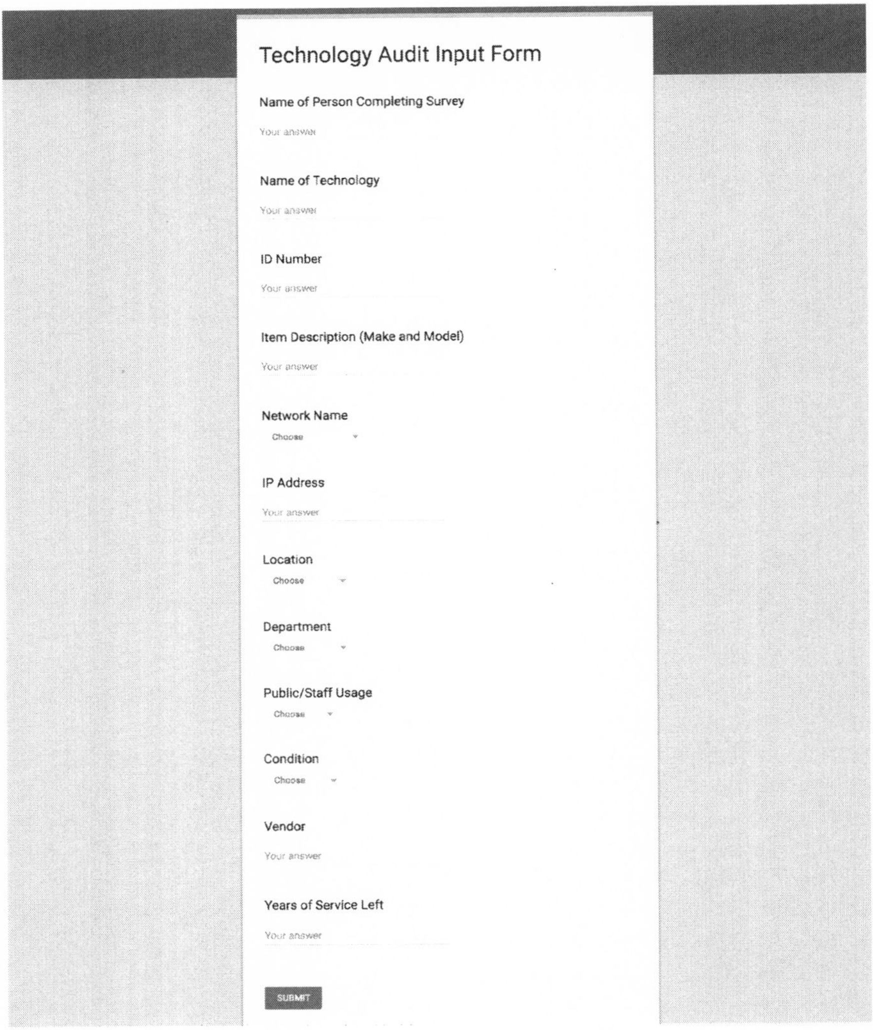

Figure 1.1. Sample survey form created with Google Forms

library that does not have a current inventory. Gentle reminders at regular intervals will help keep the assessment on track.

• Verify data. After data has been collected, send each department a spreadsheet of the data they entered for their review. They should confirm that the list is accurate and complete. If possible, the person reviewing the data should be someone different from the staff member who entered it originally, although this may not be possible if staffing is limited.

- Spot-check. To ensure your document is correct, double-check random samples. If errors or omissions are discovered, you will need to investigate further to determine if the issue is widespread. Some issues you may discover include the following:

    Fax machines or printers left off the inventory.

    Computers not properly identified. For example, a touch screen PC in the children's room may not be labeled "Touch Screen." The identifying information about touch screens is important because it affects peripherals such as keyboards and mice as well as overall use of the computers.

    Technology not assigned to a department. Some technology may fall outside a main area or may not be identified by the staff as part of the department. For example, computer stations designated for particular purposes such as genealogy or podcasting may have been left off the list. Items like these may or may not be maintained by the staff overall.

    Circulating technologies such as maker kits, e-book readers, and other items need to be inventoried, but it may not have occurred to the staff to include them.

CURRENT TECHNOLOGY: MEASURING USAGE

To document how your technology is used, you need to collect data about its usage and consider factors that may influence that use.

Statistics

Statistics about the use of your technology play a valuable role in technology planning. You need to know what is being used by the public and the staff within your library. While some statistics are easily accessible, others are more difficult to track. Sampling periods may be used to collect data from technology for which you cannot readily gather statistics on an ongoing basis.

With technology used by the public, circulation and usage statistics are likely already collected by departments; this information should be added to the audit. In addition to these, you should also consider the following:

- *Bandwidth.* Does the library's current bandwidth meet the needs of users and the staff, or are there times when demand exceeds supply? Often this data can be garnered through either logs or specialized reports via your library's firewall or network analyzer.

- *Wireless.* Is your current wireless setup working? Does it meet the needs of current users? Statistics on wireless usage will be available through your library's router. Detailed usage statistics are available based upon how many devices access the wireless network and the times of day they are in use. As part of your analysis, you will want to note both expected and unexpected peaks in usage.
- *Software.* Software includes both programs that come with your machines and those that are added later. Software can be an expensive purchase or a free program; both are supported within the library and through staff expertise. These may include programs such as Microsoft Office, résumé software, Adobe Suite, AutoCAD, or digitization software. Because specific statistics may be difficult to garner, I recommend designing a small survey to be completed over a sampling period by those who use the machines containing the specialized software.

When statistics cannot be gathered automatically, it may be necessary to collect sample statistics during a typical month. Before deciding what hardware and software to replace, update, or eliminate, you need relevant data: what is being used, and how is it used? Anecdotal evidence is not enough. Anecdotal evidence is often skewed to weigh heavily on software, technology, and users who need staff assistance. For example, if there are twenty users on public computers on a single afternoon and three users required staff assistance with résumés, the staff may report that the primary use of the computers was for résumés. In reality, only three of the twenty users (or 15 percent) used the computers for résumés that afternoon.

Sample statistics can be collected two ways. One method is to have the staff take the statistics when assisting users. However, this can be a burden on the staff and may not be truly reflective of user activity. Depending on your public access computer setup, the staff may only be interacting with those users who request assistance. The other method is for users to complete a short survey. These can be collected through a brief online questionnaire on the log-in or landing pages of specific public computers. This survey should be focused and direct, with only one or two questions that are relevant to the possible uses of that computer, such as follows:

1. What is the main purpose for which you're using this computer today?

    a. Learning a new skill
    b. Communicating with others
    c. Business
    d. Leisure

2. Will you be using specific software?

a. Microsoft Office
b. Adobe
c. Internet
d. Not sure
e. Other

Availability

As you factor statistics into the overall assessment of your current technology, you should also ascertain the actual availability of the technology. Availability may be affected by any of the following factors.

- Library hours. How is usage affected or limited by the library's hours of operation? Is the library closed evenings or on weekends? How do the hours of operation affect technology usage by school-age kids, millennials, working adults, or seniors?
- Room/equipment accessibility. Some technologies may only be available when certain areas of the library are open to the public. In some cases, specialized training is necessary before users are permitted to access hardware. This is often the case with computer labs and makerspaces. Restricted or limited access can skew overall statistics and give the impression that an item of technology is not wanted or used when the issue may actually be one of accessibility.
- Limited hardware. Notice whether statistics are maxed out. Is the item in use during every available hour? For example, if your library has only one 3-D printer or only a single computer with Photoshop software, are these used to capacity? Are users turned away, or do they face long waiting periods? Situations like these may indicate that additional technology or licenses would be well used.

Through assessment and gathering statistics, you will gain a full picture of your library's current technology.

FINAL THOUGHTS

Your library's technology assessment should not be a onetime document that is lost in a remote folder within your computer. The audit is a core part of the planning process. In chapter 4, we will discuss how to use this document to find issues and technology gaps within your library and how to consider these as you plan for the future.

The audit is not only a planning document. It should become a living document that helps you track your library's technology moving into the future. In chapter 10, we will discuss how to ensure the assessment is continually updated. For starters, I recommend creating a copy of this document and renaming it "Current Technology Inventory." Store this copy within a shared space—within a shared drive on the library's network or on a cloud-based service like Google or Dropbox—so it can be accessed by all parties who purchase, maintain, and update technology for your library.

Chapter Two

Defining Options

After identifying all current technology in your library, the next vital step in developing a good plan is to define the library's technology needs—from the staff and the community perspective. In preparing to explore those needs, it is important to familiarize yourself with technology options and trends among libraries and in the rest of the world. Understanding options and trends will help you determine the overall needs and identify the direction for the library's future technology.

LEARNING ABOUT NEW TECHNOLOGY

To learn about what's possible, look at the big picture of technical possibilities before deciding what specific technologies are appropriate for your library. There is no right or wrong answer with technology—it comes down to balancing the needs of your community and staff against your library's budget. As you work through your technology plan, it is vital to remember that technologies are just tools to help carry out and support your mission. Technology should not be purchased for technology's sake; it needs to fit into the overall picture or mission of your library.

Googling the words "current technology trends" will bring you more than two hundred million results. Such a broad search is not a good tactic for familiarizing yourself with the newest developments in the technical world. Instead, in this section we will explore some overall tips and resources for trendspotting that will assist you in focusing on the trends that are likely to affect your library over the next five years.

These four major trends of 2017 will certainly affect libraries:

- Virtual reality (VR) and augmented reality (AR)

- 3-D printing
- Threats to online security and privacy
- Software as a service (SaaS)

Let's explore each of these and what they can mean for libraries.

Virtual and Augmented Reality

Virtual and augmented realities both bring the virtual world into our physical world, but that is where their similarity ends. Virtual reality (VR) is a computer-generated, self-contained environment that immerses an individual in an alternative world or game. Popular systems include the HTC Vive, the Oculus Rift, Samsung's Gear VR, and the lower-end Google Cardboard. Those who use VR find themselves in a 360-degree world where looking up, down, and to the right or left all bring new experiences. Users can explore such diverse environments as outer space or national parks, or they can become fully immersed in a video game. Augmented reality (AR), on the other hand, layers the digital world onto the physical world. Pokemon GO, the hit game of 2016, is an example of augmented reality. While Pokemon GO and other apps bring a layer of augmented reality, the full AR experience is found in higher-end devices such as Microsoft's HoloLens, the first self-contained, holographic computer to allow users to interact with holograms in the surrounding real world.

VR and AR are outreach tools that libraries can employ. By providing development resources and offering passive and active programming, libraries are in an ideal position to introduce users to these technologies. Passive programming entails having devices available for users to explore or use with little staff guidance, while active programming includes workshops on development or guided tours of the world. Additionally, as these tools develop further, they may be used as reference resources and adaptive devices to assist users in new and exciting ways.

3-D Printing

The 3-D printing tool has been at the cusp of becoming a mainstream technology for several years. Early adopters introduced 3-D printers into libraries, often as the cornerstone of makerspaces. By 2016 there was a shift from expensive 3-D printers that cost between one and two thousand dollars to more affordable models available for less than four hundred dollars; now these devices are more accessible than ever.

Students, community tinkerers, and entrepreneurs can all use 3-D printers. Libraries are introducing users to 3-D printing by offering educational programs and by allowing dedicated blocks of time for printing and access to development resources. Three examples of 3-D printing development resources are AutoCAD, SketchUp, and Blender. While AutoCAD and Sketch-Up are subscription-based software, Blender is an open-source alternative. All three software programs allow users to create their own 3-D designs. With 3-D development resources, digitizers, and 3-D printers, libraries can be in the center of small business development, supporting individuals who are then able to design and print their prototypes for little to no cost.

Threats to Online Security and Privacy

Our devices and information are under constant threat from viruses and hackers. Libraries must protect their computer networks and equipment. They also need educated staff members who have dedicated time on a regular basis to focus on cybersecurity in order to adequately protect the network and the devices connected to it. When setting up and maintaining networks, it's important to incorporate cybersecurity measures that protect both staff and users against threats. There are three main types of threats facing libraries today.

- Ransomware. Ransomware is a computer program that encrypts and locks all files on a computer, a server, or an entire network. The files cannot be opened without a password or decryption key; the cyber attackers behind the ransomware attack then demand payment in exchange for this key. Ransomware often infects computers through a software vulnerability so it is critical to run the latest version of any software. City Library experienced a ransomware attack on one computer. Luckily, because this was a stand-alone computer used only by volunteers and not connected to the main network, the infection was contained and did not spread throughout the library's system. The computer's unique position as separate from the network had made it especially vulnerable; regular updates had not been applied, and its malware protection was outdated. As a result, everything on the computer that had not been backed up was lost. The lesson to be learned from this experience is that all technology is vulnerable and must be included in security and maintenance arrangements.
- Malware and viruses. Malware and viruses are malicious software that can run on machines or websites. The software can steal data from the browser or machine, spread to other files and devices, and otherwise cause harm to the machines and their users. The best protection from malware and viruses is antimalware software and a secure firewall.
- Data breaches. Data breaches are the result of cyberattacks via malware and phishing schemes. Nefarious individuals use malicious software to enter your network and steal data—anything from user information and passwords to credit card numbers. Protecting your network from a breach

must be in the forefront of your planning. Many data breaches start with a phishing attack. A phishing attack is when a fake email is sent to targeted individuals with the goal of soliciting the victim's password to a specific site.

Libraries must work to educate users and to protect users' personal information. Installing Deep Freeze or similar system restore software, which backs up a computer to its configured setting on each reboot, is a great start for protecting public PCs. Education campaigns to inform users about phishing threats and other security issues are also important.

Software as a Service (SaaS)

In the past, software was purchased at a onetime price. When we wanted a new edition, we had to repurchase the software. Now software is likely to be sold as a subscription for which we pay periodically; rather than owning the software, we pay to use it. The trend of developers selling "software as a service" will continue to grow. Examples of SaaS frequently found in the library realm include Office 365 and Adobe Products, among others.

The SaaS model has its pros and cons. Advantages include the following:

- Cost. Yearly/monthly fees are often lower and easier to budget than expensive purchases that can occur on an irregular basis.
- Regular updates. Vendors regularly update their software to repair bugs and security risks and to add enhancements. With SaaS, regular updates that occur automatically can free up library staff time and ensure that users always have access to the newest version of the software.
- Support. With an ongoing subscription model, the software is always under warranty. When issues arise, getting support is easier than trying to troubleshoot problems with software that is out of date.

The disadvantages of SaaS, of course, are the ongoing cost and the need for constant staff training. Sometimes there's a need for formal training; this can be the case with large updates such as the migration from Windows 8 to Windows 10. At other times, it may be sufficient to cover any training needs through small bites of instructions sent via email or through notifications of new features within the software. Either way, monitoring software updates requires dedicated staff time.

Beyond these primary trends, library technology will be affected by other developments, including the following:

- Mobile devices. As people move away from desktop computers, they rely on mobile devices as their main Internet connectors in the home environment. How will this change the ways they use library resources? Will they use desktop computers more or less when in the library? How will your library provide services to mobile users?

- Internet of things. As users adapt to the Internet of things (with all devices connected and controlled through the web), how will library services be affected? Is this an opportunity for libraries to provide services to users at home?
- Analytics. All this technology can tell us what users want and need. What information should your library collect and protect, and what should it avoid actively collecting?
- Virtual assistants and artificial intelligence. As virtual assistants such as Amazon's Echo, Apple's Siri, Microsoft's Cortana, and Google Home become more mainstream, can these devices be integrated into library services?
- E-collections. Magazine and book collections are moving online. How can we ensure library users are not lost in the digital divide?

How does understanding trends fit into the overall picture of your library? As libraries continue to evolve, they have a vital role as community centers. Your library is often where users learn about, use, and create with new technologies. Later in this chapter we will discuss defining the specific needs of your community and how emerging technologies can be used to help you reach your long-term goals for your library and community.

Keeping Up with Trends

Trendcasting—tracking trends in technology that are likely to affect your library—can be an overwhelming task if you are not naturally a technology enthusiast. Technology today changes at a quickening rate. One of the best methods for keeping abreast of these changes is to concentrate on several sources that sort through trends for you. Some good resources for libraries to follow include the following:

- LITA. The Library Information Technology Association (LITA) is a division of the American Library Association (ALA). LITA releases a list of the top ten technology trends each year during the ALA's annual conference. http://www.ala.org/lita.
- New Horizons Reports. The annual New Horizons Report, published by a consortium of educational institutions and research centers, outlines emerging technologies and how they relate to libraries, K–12 schools, and higher education. The reports contain trends along with analysis of those trends. https://www.nmc.org/nmc-horizon.

- Flipboard's Technology NewsDesk. Flipboard brings together information from multiple sources into one place for you. This particular site collects technology news. https://flipboard.com/@thenewsdesk/technology-shjum1jiz.
- Mashable. Mashable, a global multiplatform media company, is a good source for overall trend watching for technology. http://mashable.com.

Rather than signing up for email notifications from any of these sites, follow them through social media or an RSS reader such as Flipboard or Feedly. That way, you can read about technology when you have time, keeping up to date without clogging your inbox.

DEFINING NEEDS: INPUT FROM STAKEHOLDERS

In the previous section, we discussed various trends that could impact your library's technology plans for the future. However, overall trends are only relevant when they help your particular users and community. In this section, we'll focus on your library and its community along with the needs and opportunities that exist there.

Connecting Your Technology Plan to the Library

Your technology plan should be created with the library's current strategic plan or long-range plan in mind. For example, if your long-range plan identifies a need to connect to a specific stakeholder group, your technology plan should reflect that mission too. Let's say your long-range plan emphasizes expanding the library's relationship with the local small business community. In that case, your technology plan might focus on providing technology for entrepreneurs, such as the following software, facilities, and services:

- Adobe Suite
- Microsoft Office
- Small meeting rooms with tools for communication and effective meetings
- Specialized databases
- Video/photo editing and tools for creating digital marketing
- Training in the use of specialized software

If your long-range plan focuses on connecting and empowering the senior citizens who live in your community, your technology plan might include the following:

- Adaptive technology

- Tablets and tablet education classes
- Basic software for photo editing and word processing

However, it's not enough for the staff to speculate about what the community needs. Your technology plan also needs input from external sources. We will explore how to collect and understand the needs of the community as well as the needs of the staff.

Community Needs

Before asking for input from community members, assess the current and forecasted demographics for the geographic area served by your library. Considering these trends as you plan will help you set the library on a course for success in the future. Multiple resources can provide this information: census data, library databases such as Demographics Now, regional planning bodies, local realtors, chambers of commerce, and school officials.

How is your community changing, and what demographic trends are expected over the next few years? Is your community aging? Are families with young children moving in? Are neighborhoods gentrifying? Of course, overall trends do not reflect everyone's circumstances. For example, while the general trend may be toward an aging senior population, there are also families to be considered. Understanding local demographics will help focus your technology plan so that it caters to your specific community.

To help you flesh out the picture of your users, it may be helpful to create several user personas. A persona is a fictional person designed to represent a particular demographic. Having a persona helps you envision that demographic as a tangible person and can help you solicit feedback effectively from the community.

An example of a persona might be Mary, a small business owner. We can imagine Mary as follows:

- She is currently forty-two years old.
- She lives in the historic district near City Library.
- She has a four-year college degree.
- Her back story: Mary is balancing her growing cleaning service agency with raising two teenagers. She's hardworking and able to use technology, but learning new skills takes a lot of time. Therefore, much of the time she has for developing new skills is on the fly, often in the evenings.
- Mary is driven to do more but is frustrated with the need to do so with less time, especially when it comes to the logistics of promoting and running her business.

Developing a persona like this one for Mary can provide you with both a targeted look at the technology needed by this demographic and an idea of where the library can fit in. These personas can be helpful in the next steps of collecting data and understanding the user's needs. By having personas in mind, you can target specific groups with specific questions, ensure you are not missing voices when designing your data collections, and have full representation of the members of your community. A persona can help you humanize the goals and appreciate the motivations of specific demographics. For more on developing personas, I recommend visiting the Wayne State University's Guide to Patron Personas at http://guides.lib.wayne.edu/personas.

Gathering Input from Your Community

While demographics are a good start, you also need to gather community input. There are three main techniques for collecting this input: surveys, focus groups, and interviews.

Surveys

Creating a Survey   Several software tools are available to aid you in creating online surveys. If your library already has survey software, I recommend you continue using it because it likely meets your technical needs and you will not need to learn a new program. If you do not already have software, there are several options. Google offers free surveying software (google.com/forms) with a variety of question types and easy-to-manage results, giving you the ability to compile an overall analysis of the survey results. If you are looking for something even more comprehensive and that can create more versatile reports, consider Survey Monkey. It has a free version and a month-to-month subscription option; either might be adequate for your surveying needs.

Creating an effective survey is a complex process. While it's easy to list questions, it can be difficult to create questions that will get you the information you need to make effective decisions. Here are some tips for effective surveys:

- Surveys should be as short and as simple as possible. Users do not want to spend more than five minutes on a survey (and many would prefer to spend even less time). Surveys, therefore, need to be focused. While it's tempting to gather as much data as possible in a single survey, it's more important to limit the questions to only the most essential. Every question should be necessary.
- Each question should be clear and understandable to users. Avoid library jargon and any technical terms.

- A question should require only one answer. Do not include *and/or* statements. For example, you should not ask, "Do you use the public computers at the library, and what programs do you use?" Those are two distinct questions.
- Avoid question bias. Do not lead people to an answer with a question such as, "How wonderful is the library?" or, "The library has amazing resources. Do you use these great resources?"
- When structuring options for answers, avoid a simple "yes" or "no." Instead, provide responsive scales such as "strongly agree, agree, neutral, disagree, and strongly disagree." Scales will help you gauge responses more accurately.
- Limit the number of open-ended questions because they can make it difficult to reach firm conclusions. For example, a question such as, "What technology would you like to see the library offer?" is too vague; answers will be all over the place. A better approach would be to ask, "How likely are you to use Adobe Photoshop at the library?" and provide a response scale from "highly likely" to "highly unlikely."
- Remember that open-ended questions are also additional work for the respondent, so make these optional. Some people will not want to complete open-ended questions or may feel they don't know how to answer them. Place open-ended questions toward the end of the form. If the respondent doesn't answer them and completes only part of the form, you may still have some useful data. It's better to get some information rather than none.
- Always test your survey before implementing it. Ask coworkers and a few outsiders who did not work on its development to complete it. They can provide valuable input on the survey's usability and are likely to suggest changes that will make it more effective.
- Provide space on the survey for respondents to give their contact information. Some will welcome the opportunity to provide additional feedback and might be ideal choices to participate in follow-up surveys, one-on-one conversations, or future focus groups. The field for contact information should be optional.

Who Should You Survey?   Depending on which population segments you target, survey answers and results will vary. There are some groups you might want to consider for additional attention:

- *Lapsed users.* Through your integrated library system (ILS), you can gather a list of people who have not used the library for eighteen or twenty-four months. At one time these people saw value in the library, so surveying them can provide worthwhile insights into how to win them back.

- *Community at large.* This group can be difficult to reach so consider asking other community groups to distribute or promote your survey. Hearing from nonusers can often be worth the time it takes to reach them.
- *Current users.* Those who use the library often see it very differently from the way the staff sees it. Be sure to provide a method for those who visit the library in person to complete surveys. Provide links throughout your website to reach virtual users too.
- *Community leaders.* Including community leaders during your early steps of planning will help create buy-in and support as you move through developing your plan and into implementation.
- *Others.* Consider including among those surveyed any other groups of stakeholders identified in your long-range or strategic plan.

How Should You Survey?   Consider these factors when preparing a survey:

- Timing of survey
- Length of survey
- Collection period
- Survey methods

The timing of a survey is critical. For example, a public library's technology survey conducted close to back-to-school time, holidays, or large library events is likely to yield a low response. Such occasions can limit the attention and promotion that staff members or users can give to the survey.

Survey questionnaires that are dispersed primarily through email, social media, and the library's website do not need a long collection period. Online surveys can last just one week or even less. In these cases, however, it's important to remind people about the survey and to notify them of their "final chance" to complete it.

Determine whether you need supplemental paper copies of the survey available at the library or in the community. These may be necessary depending on your population. Consider paper copies if your population includes a high percentage of users with low skills in computer literacy. Note that, while distributing paper versions of the survey may increase the response rate, significant staff time will be needed to key in the results.

Another survey collection method is to assign staff or volunteers to survey users within the library—or in the community at large. Surveys can be taken via a tablet device handed to individuals. Using this technique can be tricky, though, as the collector is selecting the participants and the participants must agree to take the survey. Survey collectors need to be trained to ensure they ask a diverse group of people and include both genders and a variety of ages. In addition, the collector should not use language that would influence the survey respondent. For example, "Will you please take a moment to complete this survey so we can buy a 3-D printer" would be a leading question.

For a full picture of the community's attitudes, collect surveys at multiple points such as within different library departments, in local stores, at schools, and in other common areas within your library and its community. Failing to do so can yield results that are not representative of the community as a whole. For example, surveying only via the library's website will give you the perspective of those who use the website, but these are people who are comfortable using computers and familiar with the website; they are not likely to be representative of everyone in the community.

Focus Groups

A focus group is a facilitated small-group discussion that concentrates on specific topics. Focus groups can be extremely useful for fleshing out community needs, but they require careful planning.

The person running the focus group needs to keep participants on track, guiding their discussion through predetermined questions. The goal is to collect as much data from the attendees as possible. Decisions are not made during the focus group; information is collected for evaluation later.

When planning a focus group, consider incorporating these best practices:

- The ideal size for a focus group is five to seven individuals. While each person should represent a different user demographic, the group should be fairly homogeneous so people are comfortable.
- Keep the meeting less than an hour in length.
- Ask no more than eight to ten questions.
- It may be necessary to hold three or four focus groups where the *same* questions are asked to get responses that really represent the full range of community viewpoints.
- The facilitator's focus must be on getting individuals to speak, not on recording the outcome. Arrange for someone other than the facilitator or participants to take notes or to record the session. This will ensure accuracy and avoid any confusion over what is expressed.

Two good resources for additional information on focus groups are available online. One, "Designing and Conducting Focus Group Interviews," is on the Eastern Illinois University website (http://www.eiu.edu/ihec/Krueger-Focus-GroupInterviews.pdf). It includes a guide for those planning, leading, and evaluating focus groups along with tips on designing questions and analyzing data. A second resource is the Community Tool Box on the University of Kansas website, available at http://ctb.ku.edu.

Interviews

One-on-one interviews with key individuals can be an effective method of learning about community needs. Through talking with a spokesperson who is knowledgeable about a specific demographic or who is representative of a stakeholder group, you can crystallize thoughts and elaborate on responses collected earlier from surveys and focus groups.

When interviewing, ask each person you interview the same questions in the same manner. Individual interviews work best after you've collected data through statistics and surveys; those results will help you develop focused interview questions. For balanced responses, interview more than one person from each stakeholder group.

Determining Staff Needs

Staff needs are equally important in determining the library's technology priorities. Frontline staff members often have a clear, firsthand picture of the technological needs of library users. Those who want to use a specific technology will ask the staff for it and often ask for assistance as well. Staff members have the most experience with the library's current technology because they use the devices themselves, conduct training on it, assist users, and promote events.

To learn about the staff's perspective, develop a different survey, one that flows from the primary survey. It can also be useful to ask staff members about their own training and technology needs and about their concerns regarding the maintenance of technology.

A focus group of staff may help to clarify survey results and to brainstorm issues and concerns raised in the initial public survey of the community. The facilitator for a staff focus group should be carefully selected for two reasons. First, the facilitator needs to be able to keep the meeting on track and not allow it to become a complaint session. Second, staff members need and deserve to be heard. An outside facilitator might be warranted because staff members are often more willing to provide honest feedback to someone from outside the organization. Trained facilitators may be available through a library consortium, the state library agency, local colleges and universities, or local social service organizations like United Way.

FINAL THOUGHTS

Collecting data is easy, but collecting good data that's useful for planning your library's future takes time and thoughtful probing of the community. With varied priorities, it is important to take the time to understand the needs of your different users and their demographics. As you move forward, you will blend community needs with library and institution/city/county goals as well as with staff needs as you plan the technologies of the future.

Chapters 1 and 2 have focused on data collection. These first steps will help you lay the foundation for a strong and successful technology plan. Understanding what your library has—what is successful and why—as well as understanding what your community needs will help you determine your goals and, ultimately, define your technology plan. In the next chapter we will look at analyzing this information and at bringing it together to develop your plan.

Chapter Three

Evaluating Technology and Determining Outcomes

In the first two chapters, we focused on collecting the data necessary to create a successful technology plan. We saw that the first step in creating that plan is conducting an assessment that establishes a clear picture of the technology on hand and how it is used. A second, equally vital, step is to collect input on the technology needs of both the library staff and your community. In chapter 3, we start working through the results of both the audit of existing technology and the staff and community feedback to make sense of the data collected. From this, we will compile an actual list of goals and outcomes.

Here is one piece of advice to remember as you begin this important part of the project: avoid going through the process solo. Analyzing the data that has been gathered is a difficult and time-consuming task. The ideal team for this task is a small working group of two to four members selected from different parts of the library. A team approach is an effective way to analyze data, make decisions, and create your technology plan. Involving several key people will make the planning process more efficient and will result in a more complete and useful document.

Who should be on this team? That will depend on your library and on the abilities of your staff, but you will certainly want to have several voices represented. Some staff members might be able to represent more than one of these voices. Areas to consider for representation include the following:

- Reference staff. Reference staff members interact daily with users. They know what resources are often needed or requested and know which technology items are currently used.

- Tech services. This department will have ultimate responsibility for deploying and maintaining any new technology; its members should have input into the technology plan.
- Youth services. Those who work in youth services see a completely different segment of the population from those who work exclusively in adult services; they will have distinct ideas on which technologies should have priority and how they should be implemented.
- Management. In the final analysis, those responsible for library administration must approve the technology plan. It is essential that this plan match the library's overall mission and its long-term plan for services. Having a representative of the management team to speak for the library's mission is vital for buy-in by the administration and for the ultimate success of the plan.

Other characteristics to consider when looking for staff to include on the technology planning committee or work group include the following:

- Influencers. Influencers are those individuals who can help create buy-in and excitement among the rest of the staff. They are not necessarily administrators or managers. Technology-forward staff members often can bring ideas and solutions that are on the forefront of technology.
- Early adopters. Early adopters, or innovators, are those who are among the first to try new technologies, so they often know of technologies on the cusp of general interest. Early adopters can help present newer technologies for consideration in the plan.
- Decision makers. Many decisions need to be made, and they should be made efficiently. The person who chairs the technology planning committee must be empowered to help the team make decisions. Further, the team must be willing to commit to decisions once they are made.

There are additional benefits of a team approach. This method can help provide buy-in since all staff members will know there were staff voices at the planning table. Team members can also help communicate the plan's development, creating a more transparent planning process. Without buy-in and a sense of transparency, the decisions that contribute to the technology plan may not be understood, resulting in miscommunication or a feeling that some departments were overlooked or others shown favoritism. For example, a decision to place a new 3-D printer in the adult services department could cause resentment among those who work with youth or teens. Using a team approach, however, can help keep the process transparent by making the reasoning clear and by addressing issues of access for everyone early in the process.

ANALYZING YOUR TECHNOLOGY ASSESSMENT

Let's start our data analysis by analyzing your technology audit. In this section, we'll cover two ways to work with the spreadsheet where data on existing technology was collected. We'll consider the value of creating a visual map and then we'll start listing the issues and gaps as they are identified.

Creating a Visual Map

During your audit, you used a spreadsheet to capture data about your library's current technology setup. You can take that spreadsheet data and turn it into a visual map.

A visual map has several benefits. Visualizing data makes it easier to see trends that might be missed when simply scanning a spreadsheet. A visual map displays the data and shows how it interrelates, highlighting how one aspect of technology connects to other technologies.

Creating a visual map is a way to understand your current technology better and is a good place to start identifying the gaps between needs and existing resources. A visual map should be created for each department or branch for larger libraries, or for the entire organization if your library is smaller. If the library system is too large to complete a visual map for the entire system, you might highlight a few, selected departments, focusing on those with the greatest needs for technology.

Visual mapping is done with software. While specialized software is available, it's not essential. Possible options include the following:

- Microsoft Office or Publisher. Most libraries have one or both of these programs that can be used with clip art (from sources like Flaticon.com or openclipart.org) and text boxes to create visual representations of a system, a branch, or a department.
- Mind Vector (mindvectorweb.com for Android or Apple iOS). Available via the web or on your tablet or phone, this flexible software allows data to be easily exported as an image or downloaded into comma-separated value (CSV) format ready to import into a spreadsheet.
- LucidChart (lucidchart.com). LucidChart offers easy-to-use templates for creating network maps that depict a visual representation of a specific area.
- Bubbl (bubbl.us). This program provides the ability to download a map in HTML, which is a benefit when sharing the information on the web or an intranet. Bubbl is available as freeware, but the added features of its paid version allow downloading visual maps, real-time collaboration, and a revision history.

- Spreadsheet graphs. Simple visual representations can be made through the graph-producing feature of Excel or alternative spreadsheet software. This works especially well when displaying responses to survey questions that used drop-down menus or offer multiple-choice answers.

Take a look at figure 3.1, a sample visual map that was created in Microsoft Word for Beach Library, a branch of the Unity Library System. This map lays out the technology within the entire branch. Additional, alternative versions of the map could be created to focus on single departments. The visual representation uses two-way arrows to demonstrate how technology is connected to the different networks. In addition, the technology is shown as grouped into basic categories: peripherals, computers, and other devices. While the data depicted does not present all the information in the spreadsheet, the visualization helps create a snapshot of how technology is arranged in the library.

With a visual map, you can see that Beach Library has gaps in its technology regarding the operating systems of both staff and public computers. For example, one glaring issue is that not all computers are using the same operating system. One important technology goal for this library would be to have all computers on the latest operating system. Each computer that's

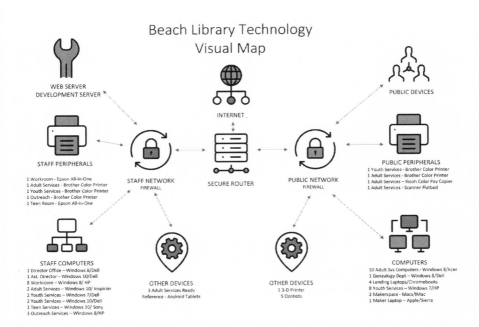

Figure 3.1. Visual map of Beach Library's current technology

currently using an older, lower version should be analyzed to determine whether a simple update can bring the machine up to the current version, or whether that machine should be replaced with a new computer that has improved memory and processing power. Other gaps that may become visible when technology is represented visually include out-of-date technology such as fax machines that are not being maintained; areas without access to printers; and areas that did not receive new computers in the last round of upgrades.

Visual maps will also be of help later in the planning process and when working with funding and funders. The visual representation of technology gaps can make a striking impact in an easy-to-understand format.

Identifying Issues and Creating an Issues List

Now we will start looking for trends in your technology assessment. As you went through the audit process, what issues did you notice? You probably spotted many concerns during your review. Start a list of these. Include potential security issues and usability issues too. Also, identify areas in which technology may be lacking. For example, if there is no staff computer in the teen room but it would be helpful to have one there, note that on your list. Does your library have multiple floors? If so, is there adequate technology available, for both users and staff, on each floor? Is the equipment located on the floor or in the department where it is most needed for effective utilization? Think about what could be done differently. For example, if it's not practical to have desktop computers for the staff on each floor or in each area of the library because of space or other building constraints, would tablets be a more appropriate solution?

To track the list of issues, I recommend using a spreadsheet. Useful columns for this spreadsheet include basic identifying information such as the library branch or department, the identified technology, and the action needed. Specific actions to consider include the following:

- Software upgrade. Is a new version of the software available?
- Security. Is the device secure, both physically and in terms of its operation? Does security software need to be installed or updated? Are there vulnerabilities—software or physical—that need to be addressed? Is this technology subject to theft? Does it need to be physically secured in some way?
- Replace or discard technology. Is the technology woefully old, out of date, or in chronic need of repair? It might be time to replace or even discard the device. As devices approach the end of their useful lives, they will develop an increasing number of problems, such as shortened battery life, inability to load new updates, limits exceeded on memory storage, slow load

times, and applications that fail to work. When a device approaches the end of its useful life, you must decide whether a new device is warranted or whether the old device should simply be eliminated. The answer will vary depending on the technology's purpose. As an example, consider an older tablet. Tablets and mobile devices normally have a lifespan of five to six years. If the tablets are used for roaming reference or for user training, they're likely to still be needed and should be replaced. Perhaps they were purchased to assist with downloading e-books for users, for some special in-house use, or for a particular project or program. Does that need still exist? If these tablets are no longer being used, maybe they just need to be withdrawn. Keeping old technology, just for the sake of saying you have that technology, can drain the resources of your IT department and can often give users a substandard library experience.

As you evaluate your current technology, look for the following issues:

- Version control with software
- Compatibility of devices
- Security
- Obsolescence or hardware that is approaching the end of its useful life

Let's explore each of these issues, identifying what you should look for as you determine the condition and usefulness of each item.

Version Control with Software

Are some of the library's computers older than others? Are similar computers, which may be located in different branches or departments, running different software versions? Sometimes there's a tendency to neglect software updates or even a deliberate decision to skip updates, thinking that moving to a new version would be too difficult or might require too much training of the staff or users. I visited one library that had recently purchased new computers with the Windows 8 operating system instead of using this opportunity to transition to Windows 10; I strongly recommend against this practice. Do not avoid new technology. Technology will not move backward. When you reject the opportunity to upgrade your technology, you are providing your users with an obsolete system and making adoption even harder in the long run. Therefore, your list of issues should include any computers not running the most up-to-date software version available.

Compatibility of Devices

Keep in mind the importance of device compatibility—the way in which devices interact with each other and the specifications necessary for this to occur smoothly. For example, the projector in your community room or small business area must be able to connect to the laptop computers your library uses, both now and in the future. Does the projector require a VGA, HDMI, or USB connector to receive the data to be projected? Similarly, does the computer to be used with the projector need a CD-ROM drive, a DVD drive, or a USB drive to play content? Does the device need to be upgraded or replaced to fit with current technology? As you plan for technology updates, make sure devices can connect natively, that is, they are designed to work with any equipment that must be connected to them. If connections are not native, is an adaptor available? You do not want to purchase new equipment that will require multiple work-arounds to function with your other technology.

How will users access their own content on a library computer? Will they be able to download content to computers and tablets from the cloud or access that content via flash drives? Some forms of access, such as CD-ROMs or DVDs, are considered older technologies and often are no longer standard items on new computers. Be sure to study hardware specifications carefully because many laptops sold today are not equipped with ports for flash drives or projector cables and may require special adaptors.

Security

Did your technology audit reveal any security vulnerabilities? Every computer should be running up-to-date security software that protects against viruses, malware, and ransomware. Any computers without such protection are vulnerable. Further, have all the peripheral devices connected to the library's network been approved for this purpose, and are those peripherals also running current versions of their operating software?

The network itself is another area to analyze for security. Are both public and staff computers on the same network? That can create a significant security risk. Are the library's own technology devices connected to the correct network? A best practice for network security is to establish a firewall between staff and public devices, segregating the two into separate, secure zones. The router can be used to create two such zones. The network zones required may vary according to your library's needs, but at a minimum, there should be a private network for staff and a separate public network. Additional networks may be added for publicly accessible technology, for administrative computers, and for different departments. Separate networks not only create a secure environment and manage accessibility to devices and resources; they also help distribute bandwidth more effectively.

Additional best network practices to consider and discuss with your IT staff may include centralized software management, authenticating staff computers via their media access control (MAC) addresses, and prohibiting the use of unauthorized devices.

Explore establishing a centralized software management system if you do not already have one in place. A centralized system lets you control software updates and manage permissions across your network. It also allows monitoring of network traffic and can be integrated into an intrusion detection system to further harden security. An intrusion detection system will alert IT staff to unwanted network traffic, policy violations, or malicious activity. One example of a centralized system is Microsoft's Active Directory (https://www.microsoft.com), which allows the library to identify at-risk workstations and then force security updates to those locations. Management of workstations can be done remotely, an especially attractive feature for library systems with multiple branches. There are also open-source alternatives, such as OpenLDAP (https://www.openldap.org). Open-source alternatives are free and can be as good as or even better than their paid counterparts. On the other hand, open-source solutions do not offer the same level of technical support because the support is via the user community instead of the company. With open source, any further development or customization of software comes from the community of users or from your own staff. To ensure success, libraries choosing open-source software management systems must have the staff with the technical know-how to manage it.

For added protection, each staff computer should be authenticated via its MAC address, not with just a simple log-in. The MAC address is a unique identifier for each device on the network. Machines for staff use, those that are allowed on the staff-only network, should be set up and authenticated through the router. The public side of the network should remain as open as possible, but it also needs a strong, well-maintained program of antivirus and malware protection.

On the staff network, there should be no unauthorized devices. For example, personal hotspots and cell phones should not be allowed to connect to the staff network due to the security risk they represent. Unauthorized devices can open an otherwise secure network to unwanted traffic, viruses, and other malware. As an alternative, staff members may connect their devices to the open public network.

Obsolescence or End-of-Life Hardware

Hardware eventually reaches the end of its life. Waiting for computers, printers, or other technical equipment to die before replacing them is not a productive policy. Such a reactionary approach, under which replacements are only purchased when their predecessors die, can cost more than replacing technology systematically. Additional costs can arise from replacing equipment in urgent circumstances, purchasing in a rush, or lacking the time to find the best deals. Purchasing hardware as a reaction versus following a planned approach can monopolize staff time, and further, doing so delivers a lower level of customer service.

There are several indicators that hardware is reaching the end of its life.

- Operating system. Obsolete software that is no longer supported by the vendor is a leading security issue.
- Maintenance problems. As hardware ages, its need for maintenance grows. If a device develops repeated and increasing maintenance problems, its end of life may be near.
- Age. Technology ages and becomes less capable of performing the functionality needed. Computers slow down, and new devices will often have greater capacities than earlier versions.

Determine the official end-of-life date for all the hardware in your library. Some organizations decide that the end should be when the technology's maintenance contract expires. TechSoup, the nonprofit known for helping libraries and nongovernmental organizations with technology tools and solutions, recommends the following: "In general, desktop systems and servers are replaced every three to four years, while laptops, phones and other mobile devices are swapped every two to three years. Printers and networking equipment may last five years or more" (TechSoup n.d.).

Textbox 3.1. Technology Assessment Questions

As you analyzed your technology audit, what gaps did you identify? What needs exist that are not being addressed by the current technology resources? What surprised you in the data collection?

Analyzing Community and Staff Input

After analyzing your audit to identify technology gaps, the next step is to analyze the data collected from surveys, focus groups, and interviews with community members and the staff.

If you conducted surveys and focus groups, then you have a lot of data to review. First, summarize the data and look for overall trends. Questions that were created in multiple choice or drop-down formats will be easy to tally. Most types of survey software are also able to produce a visual representation of the data from questions of this type.

"Free-form" answers, where users typed sentences or paragraphs, are more difficult to assess. I recommend grouping the free-form responses into defined categories and placing comments where they fit. For example, you may have asked an open-ended question such as, "Do you have any addition-

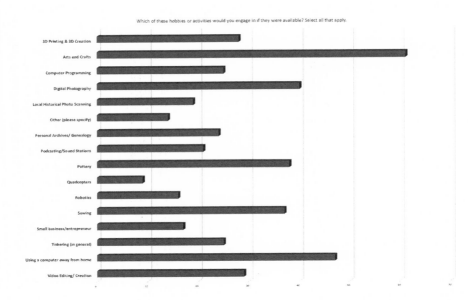

Figure 3.2. Responses from library users surveyed regarding technology for new maker areas at Beach Library

al comments about how Unity Library System can do a better job with technology to help you achieve your goals?" For typical answers to this question, you might decide to sort responses into these categories: increase hours of operation; provide faster Internet; add more classes; and circulate more technology. Comments that do not fit these established categories should be placed into an "other" category and analyzed on their own; they definitely should not be discounted. Remember, though, that a comment is just one person's response and therefore should not be weighed heavier than other responses or information received from different sources.

Once again, before you delve into specific replies and insights, create a visual representation of the data to reveal overall trends. For example, Beach Library used SurveyMonkey to conduct a community survey to help plan their upcoming makerspace. They expected a lot of interest from the public in 3-D printing, robotics, and other cutting-edge technologies. However, as you can see from the survey results dramatically displayed in figure 3.2, community members responded emphatically that they were more interested in other forms of technology—such as crafts, photography, and sewing— than in small business resource centers and quadcopters.

Staff responses should be analyzed with the same time, energy, and weight given to public surveys. Staff members need to be heard and to have their ideas incorporated into the plan if they are to buy in to the final result.

Without their buy-in, there will be additional obstacles to implementing and promoting any new technology within the library.

Textbox 3.2. Discussion Questions

What trends are you seeing in requests or stated needs from your community? From your staff? How are they similar? Where do they differ?

The questions raised in the pull-out box should be discussed within your library and especially within the planning committee. It is important to understand which needs are universal (i.e., those needs important to both staff and community) and to note where and why the needs of staff and community members diverge.

Watch for any community (or staff) requests for services that are already provided. Don't simply dismiss these comments because they seem redundant. For example, perhaps you received responses asking for "computer classes," "tablets," "3-D printing," or some other technology the library already provides. Why are people requesting services that are already available? This is an important question to investigate. Possible answers include the following:

- Lack of promotion. How is this technology or service promoted? Who is your target audience? Is the target audience being reached? Should you be marketing this service in different ways?
- Lack of visibility. Where is the technology located within the library? Finding space for equipment can be a challenge. Sometimes space limitations cause incredible resources to be tucked away from users' normal paths through the library. A small meeting lab for entrepreneurs might have been located in an out-of-the-way nook or repurposed office space where its meeting software, laptops with specialized software, and other tools haven't been discovered by intended users. If key technology is housed in spaces like this, effective marketing is essential to make its existence abundantly clear. Appropriate signage is also necessary to identify the location. Users will not know to ask for something if they do not expect to find it or even know about its existence.
- Lack of proximity. Technology may only be offered at a certain location or in a particular department and not at the branch or areas of the library a user frequents. Is the only 3-D printer in the teen room or at the main branch? Situations like this are inevitable, especially with expensive technologies. Find ways to make sure everyone who needs access to the technology knows where it is located and has an opportunity to use it.

- Limited access. Does the area where the technology is housed have incon-
venient hours? Similarly, does the technology live in a staff-only area that
is only accessible during programs or with staff assistance or supervision?
Restricted hours in these special areas are often due to staffing limitations,
but the result may be that certain user groups are excluded. These restrictions become barriers that can limit access. For example, is the makerspace only open during the day or available only on weekdays? Hobbyists
are most likely to utilize makerspaces on nights and weekends, while
entrepreneurs need access during the day and students need it after school.

Analyzing Statistical Data

As part of your assessment, you will want to examine any statistics gathered
on the use of technology within the library. Each type of technology and each
technology area should be analyzed to determine overall trends. Usage statistics can provide a more complete picture than anecdotal evidence alone. Data
to be reviewed should include the following:

- Internet. Is the current bandwidth adequate to meet the needs of all users?
Are response times slow because bandwidth maxes out, indicating you're
reaching the limits of your network? Are there usage peaks on specific
routers or networks? When do they occur? What causes these peaks? Does
it appear that additional bandwidth is needed now or in the foreseeable
future?
- Computer usage. Is usage increasing? Decreasing? How are people using
the computers? Are certain computers, or those in certain departments,
being used more than others? What would the reason be?
- Software. Are statistics on the use of software and databases within the
library available to you? If so, which software is being used most? Does
identifying the software that's in demand provide insight into your users'
needs?
- Other technologies. What other technologies do you offer? Are they being
used? If so, to what extent? Do you need to expand that type of technology? If not, why not? For example, if you have a podcast station, is it being
used most of the day, or are there times when it is idle? Heavy use might
indicate a need for additional stations, either in the same area or in a
different department or location. If new equipment is not an option, would
a different setup with multiple pieces of equipment create more opportunities for use? On the flip side, is this station not being used? Why not?
Are there barriers to access such as lack of availability, staffing, or training? Is the station's availability being marketed properly? Do its features
fit the needs of your community?

Analyzing the List

Once the gaps and requests have been compiled into a list, then the team should determine how it will identify technologies to address those needs.

It is easy to get lost in the details when working on a technology plan. Be sure to notice the larger trends as well as the specifics. Keep in mind the entire picture of your technology. In other words, don't just focus on individual trees; from time to time, be sure to zoom out and view the entire forest. It may be tempting to fixate on specific devices or brands at this point, but pay attention to broader trends. Considering the technology interests and changes occurring in your community, in the nation, and around the world will help determine the services your library needs to provide. Examples of current trends include the following:

- STEAM education support. STEAM (science, technology, engineering, art, and mathematics) is a major trend in primary and secondary schools, colleges, and beyond. Libraries are often on the forefront in providing resources to help students and adult learners explore ideas, develop critical thinking skills, and prepare for a changing job market.
- Innovative technologies. Innovative technologies are those on the cusp, just beginning to emerge. Some may not yet be available for general purchase or their cost may be prohibitive for individuals or classrooms. Often libraries can introduce these technologies to the community. By making them available, libraries are able to help small businesses that may need these resources but can't afford to purchase them. Libraries are also in an ideal position to expose community members to life-changing technologies such as tools for augmented or virtual reality.
- Small business/entrepreneurial tools. Members of the small business community are a core group of public library users. Owners of small businesses and their staffs use the library to create products, develop business plans, and run more effective businesses using tools they cannot afford on their own. Libraries may function as small business hubs by focusing on four main areas.

    Prototype development. By offering expensive equipment that individuals may only need occasionally, libraries provide a much-needed service. Examples of such equipment include 3-D printers, sewing machines, and laser cutters.

    Marketing. Resources to enable entrepreneurs to market a product or service might include video, HD, and 360-degree cameras; Adobe Suite; video and photo editing software; and web development assistance.

    Business development. Resources for development may include physical space within the library designed to meet the needs of small business owners, specialized databases and other business-oriented tools, and programming.

Small meeting rooms. Meeting space that is furnished with sharing technologies such as meeting software and collaboration tools is a valuable resource for small businesses.

- Job training. As job markets change, users look to the library as a place where they can learn new technology-focused skills.
- Hardware and software. Those who are learning to use new technologies and are building a basic foundation for digital literacy need fundamental tools for computing.

SETTING GOALS

Fitting the Technology Plan into the Library's Overall Long-Term Goals

Your technology plan is not in a silo, isolated from the rest of the library's operation. It must incorporate the goals of the library and address the needs of your community. As you review feedback from all your stakeholders, see whether the overall trends found there match your library's long-term goals. Are there differences? If so, where are they and what caused them? There might be good reasons the two plans show different priorities. Have there been changes in the community? Have community needs shifted over time? Did the long-term plan miss an important or emerging need? Did the long-term goals lack a technology component?

Fortunately, the community analysis conducted for technology planning often overlaps substantially with the library's long-term goals. For example, a need to serve the small business community that emerges during planning for technology will likely match up with long-range goals that address helping local businesses and organizations thrive.

What Technology Gaps Need to Be Addressed?

Did your assessment and community inquiries reveal areas where the library lacks appropriate technology or where existing technology should be upgraded? At Beach Library, for example, computers were using different operating systems, and several machines lacked basic security software. In your library, are there departments where some machines missed upgrades, have only older computers, or lack any computers at all? Are some specific user groups underserved or even unserved? Some demographics can be underserved inadvertently, so look at each demographic closely. Some groups that can easily be underserved include those with low computer literacy, hobbyists, kids, and teens.

What Technology Needs Do You Foresee in Your Community?

In chapter 2, we discussed analyzing the demographics of the area served by your library and the ways in which this area is changing. Did your research reveal trends for which you need to prepare? For example, is your community experiencing a shift in population from retirees to younger families? Similarly, is the education level in your community high or low, and is this level beginning to change? What new or different technologies will be needed as these changes unfold?

CREATING GOALS AND OUTCOMES

Different libraries, even those geographically close to each other, will have different goals. Each library's goals depend on its specific community, the resources of its library, and the attitudes of its community leaders. Goals are not a one-size-fits-all proposition. Instead, goals must be individualized. Although your technology plan should identify goals specific to your library, they should fit into the broader picture. We will discuss some sample goals and their related outcomes. Examples of overall goals for a technology plan may include the following:

- Improve the library's infrastructure.
- Provide support to the library's small business community.
- Bring innovative technology to the library staff and the community.
- Standardize and boost user support for technologies within the library.

Keep in mind that, unlike outcomes, goals are not measurable. Therefore, your plan will need more specifics than just generalized statements like the ones above. For improvements to become reality, each goal must have outcomes and actions. For example, the first goal listed above, "Improve the library's infrastructure," might have the following accompanying outcomes:

- Upgrade and update computers to current versions by the end of the current fiscal year.
- Optimize the library's current bandwidth this year, and increase bandwidth as needed to meet demand.

These outcomes can be broken down further into singular actions like "upgrade software on reference computers" and "purchase two new computers for the youth services department" for the first goal and "update the router" and "configure and utilize router to maximize bandwidth" for the second.

The last sample goal, "Standardize and boost user support for technologies within the library," will be the impetus for outcomes related to staff development as you bring new technologies and standards to your library.

PRIORITIZING NEEDS

In order to create goals and outcomes, figuring out your library's priorities is key. After considering technology gaps, staff requests, and community feedback, you will have a long list of technologies that are needed or desired. Prioritization will ensure that the most urgent needs are addressed first and will help you find ways to reach your goals as efficiently as possible. For example, your library may need to add a new computer lab or makerspace. Implementing this might not be possible within the current budget, but it is a goal toward which you can begin planning immediately. It may be necessary to delay a new lab until later in the plan, but updating the computers in a specific department or branch or purchasing basic makerspace technologies are tasks that likely could be accomplished right away. That will lay the foundation for a more expansive arrangement in the second or third year of your plan.

Your technology plan should focus on a time frame of three to five years. Identify what needs to be implemented within the current fiscal year, the second year, and so forth. The technology planning team should consider prioritizing tasks based on

- the gap to be filled by the technology under consideration;
- how this technology relates to the library's long-range plan;
- how the need for this technology was ranked by the community and the staff; and
- how the technology fits within your budgeting.

This prioritizing process is most easily done by your technology planning group. After a priority has been assigned to each item on the list, you and your team will be able to determine the direction for your technology plan.

FINAL THOUGHTS

Evaluating your library's assessment and community needs will help you develop the goals and outcomes for your technology plan. These goals and outcomes will relate directly to the new technologies you plan to bring to your library. By tying technology to specific goals, everyone—staff, community, and stakeholders—can understand which community needs the technologies will fulfill. Having a solid plan with concrete goals helps funders and decision makers understand why a given technology is necessary and how it will benefit the library and community. As you implement your technology plan, these outcomes will determine a roadmap to success.

Chapter Four

Selecting Technology and Developing Your Technology Plan

Identifying the needs of your community and your library and developing overall goals and outcomes for the library's technology services will help you design an effective technology plan. Chapter 4 explores the tasks that will comprise your plan—the nitty-gritty of selecting the actual technology, preparing for its installation, formulating a timeline for implementation, and creating a budget for acquiring the technology while minimizing any unexpected costs.

SELECTING AND EVALUATING TECHNOLOGY

Think of the plan's goals and outcomes as your destination. This chapter will help you create a roadmap for reaching that destination. With individualized goals for your library and a prioritized list of technology issues to be resolved and new technologies to be added, you are ready to begin the detailed work of selecting solutions and preparing a budget.

Reviews for Hardware and Software

As you seek technology solutions to meet the needs on your issues list, begin by identifying specific products and determining prices. Although some products may be well known and appropriate entities, it's vital to read current reviews and to understand the value you'll receive when making technology purchases. Some good places to find reviews include the following:

- Amazon. Even if you are not purchasing from Amazon, the site posts a large collection of reviews from verified purchasers, an important consideration.
- Computer magazines and other specialized topic magazines. These are especially helpful when considering special-purpose equipment. For example, if you are setting up a visual editing station for video, video-focused magazines will have reviews of appropriate software. Use your library databases to find and access the reviews you need.

In addition to reading reviews, I strongly recommend using the manufacturer's trial period to test unfamiliar software before buying it. During the trial, ask the staff and selected users to experiment with the software and to provide detailed feedback on the following:

- Usability. How easy or intuitive is it to use? If a feature is hard to find or difficult to utilize, that feature does not offer much benefit.
- Performance. Does the software do what you need?
- Quality of product. Are there "bugs" or other problems with the software?
- Support. How responsive is the company's support team? Is the help that you need available when you need it? Does the software or its community offer tutorials or an FAQ section to help you understand all of the product's functionality?
- Quality of final product. Does this product offer the best solution for the price?

Selecting Computers

When buying computers, there are four main considerations: central processing unit (CPU); random access memory (RAM); storage, alternatively known as the hard disk; and video cards. Depending on how a computer will be used, the specific requirements for each of these four factors may vary. For example, a teen room computer that will be used for gaming will need significantly more CPU, RAM, and storage than a computer used for general Internet access by the public. Gaming, conference, and video editing machines will all benefit from higher-performance video cards. Costs escalate greatly with higher-end PCs, so it is vital that you identify the computer's purpose before making a purchase.

Servers

When selecting a computer to be used as a server, consider these factors before making a purchase.

- What will the server be used for?

- How many users is the server expected to support?
- Do you have the in-house expertise to maintain a server?
- Do you have dedicated space to house the server?
- Should you consider a cloud server solution?

A cloud server is a virtual server hosted by a third-party company. There are multiple options for virtual servers including flexible server space, private servers, and shared platforms. There is not a one-size-fits-all solution, and multiple cloud options might be appropriate for your library depending on your needs.

A cloud-based or virtualized IT infrastructure can have several advantages.

- The library does not need to manage the infrastructure for servers or to provide dedicated space for a server within its building.
- The resiliency and redundancies of cloud-based servers can add some depth to disaster planning because these servers are often located throughout the world.
- Virtualized servers may offer levels of security that many in-house library servers cannot replicate.

For a virtualized solution to be successful, it is vital to understand your server requirements in advance. While many arrangements allow for scalability, it is important to understand the costs, risks, and limitations of cloud servers before moving forward. This is especially true with large-scale implementations for which the cost of cloud servers can increase drastically.

Buying Other Hardware

When planning hardware purchases, keep an open mind about which vendors to choose. Watch for sales by big box stores and for closeouts from places like Apple. Slightly older models of tablets, printers, and other hardware can often run the newest software while offering a steep discount from the prices of the newest models. As you evaluate additional hardware, keep the following questions in mind.

- Are there ongoing costs associated with this hardware? What are those costs, and what are the options? For instance, a traditional printer requires ink while a 3-D printer requires filament. How will the library budget for these recurring expenses? Different printer models handle ink and filament differently. Do you have to purchase supplies from the manufacturer, or are there other third-party options?

- What functionality do you require? As discussed in previous chapters, be careful to determine your true needs, and don't just compile a wish list for new hardware.
- What ongoing maintenance will the hardware require? Will this be handled internally, by the vendor, or by a third party?

Maintenance, Warranties, and Service Plans

For some products, selecting an extended warranty or adding a maintenance plan might be a good idea. To decide, consider these questions.

- What is the product's expected life span?
- Does the basic warranty cover the product's expected life span?
- What avenues of support are provided? Some products come with free support through community forums. Others provide support through email, chat, or phone. A number of vendors offer different tiers of support with different pricing models. Your library's comfort level on the support issue may vary depending on the technology. For example, most libraries will require fast, almost instantaneous support for a large, high-demand public printer. On the other hand, support that's less immediate—such as that provided by email or a forum—may be acceptable for certain types of software.
- What is the technological skill level of your library staff? Do you have employees who can troubleshoot and resolve issues, or will the vendor be the sole source of support?
- Will you need to purchase a maintenance or service plan to keep the product running? Some types of equipment, such as large printers, often require staff with specialized training to troubleshoot and maintain them.
- Is there an extended maintenance or service plan option? Would this option be cost effective for your library? Would it expand the lifespan of the product for your library?
- Does your library or parent institution (e.g., city, county, or school system) have maintenance policies you must follow?

If you are buying multiple computers from one vendor, arranging for support is a key negotiation point and may prove as valuable as the overall discount.

Free Alternatives for Software

While software is available for purchase, there are other options to explore as well. These include open-source and freeware alternatives.

Open-source software is freely available and robust. It's often as (or even more) sophisticated than the familiar commercial versions. The community of open-source users contributes to enhancements and provides troubleshooting. But support is only available through the open-source community; the thoroughness and accuracy of the support is not guaranteed. Updates and upgrades can be irregular and no maintenance contracts are available. Some software (especially complex systems like open-source integrated library systems) can require significant specialized staff to keep it up and running.

Beyond true open-source options, your library may be able to utilize freeware or "light" versions of software. Freeware is software offered free of charge by companies and nonprofits. A popular example of freeware is Google Drive. Other examples of software with light versions include Slack for team communication and Dropbox for cloud storage of files. Note that light versions often lack the full functionality of paid versions and can contain advertising or bloatware (unwanted added software).

Popular Open-Source and Freeware Software to Consider

- Security. There are several options for open-source antimalware and antivirus software including ClamAV (https://www.clamav.net) and AdAware (https://www.adaware.com).
- Web platforms. Developing a website for your library, for a specific program within the library, or for a staff intranet can be done easily without a lot of coding knowledge using a content management system (CMS). The two most popular open-source solutions are Drupal (https://www.drupal.org) and WordPress (https://wordpress.org).
- Office suites. There are alternatives to Microsoft Office. Libre Office (https://www.libreoffice.org) is a computer-based open-source alternative and Google Drive (https://www.google.com/drive) is a cloud-based solution.
- Web browsers. Firefox, from Mozilla (https://www.mozilla.org/en-US/firefox), is an open-source browser available for PC, Mac, and mobile devices. It focuses on user privacy and is an alternative to Microsoft and Google browsers.
- 3-D design and graphics. Blender (https://www.blender.org) is multimedia content creation software that allows users to create 3-D graphics and designs.
- Photo editing. GIMP (https://www.gimp.org) is a photo-editing software package that allows for advanced photo and graphic creation and editing. In terms of features, it's often compared to Adobe Photoshop.
- Operating systems. Linux (https://www.ubuntu.com) is an alternative operating system, one that might be desirable when reusing older machines that cannot run Windows.
- Communication tools. Google Hangouts (https://hangouts.google.com) and Slack (https://slack.com) are tools that can enable staff to communi-

cate quickly and effectively at every service point and through mobile devices.

Library-Specific Open-Source Software

- Evergreen (https://evergreen-ils.org) is an open-source integrated library system (ILS).
- Koha (http://www.koha.org) is an open-source ILS system for libraries.
- VuFind (https://vufind.org/vufind) is a discovery layer that can be added to your ILS in order to create a custom user experience.

BUYING TECHNOLOGY

When buying technology and related items, you will need to follow the procedures laid out by your library or parent organization. Your institution may have contracts with specific companies or require bids. It is important to stay in line with existing policies. However, if you have some flexibility, there are options.

- Deal directly with the vendor. Look for bulk rates when buying multiple licenses or devices.
- Look for nonprofit and education rates. If you don't see these listed on the vendor's website, call and ask. Many companies offer software to libraries at a discount. When looking for these discounts, think creatively. If a vendor only provides discounts to organizations with a 501(c)(3) designation from the Internal Revenue Service, a possible solution might be to have your Friends of the Library organization or library foundation make the purchase; the library can then reimburse the purchaser.
- Check with TechSoup (http://techsoup.org), a nonprofit network that provides technology tools and support and that offers libraries significant discounts on software and hardware.
- Look at both big box stores and online retailers to compare costs.
- Evaluate whether you can use items you already have, especially furniture.
- Can you build it? You may have community members, city or county facilities staff members, or library staff members who are capable of building or repurposing furniture. If the area to be added will be a type of makerspace, a building project is a great way to jump-start the new project.

ASSISTIVE TECHNOLOGY

Assistive technology, a term for devices that enhance the capabilities of people, can change lives. Assistive technologies vary greatly and have been developed to meet a variety of needs for those with different disabilities ranging from blindness to hearing loss and mobility impairment. Assistive technology varies from screen readers and magnifiers for those with low vision to more complex technology, including alternatives to traditional mice and keyboards for people with coordination challenges. Choices in assistive technology depend on the library's user base and on community needs.

Under federal law, all electronic and information technology procured, maintained, or used by the federal government must be accessible to people with disabilities. Specific requirements are described in Section 508, an amendment to the United States Workforce Rehabilitation Act of 1973. In addition to adding adaptive tools, your library's online resources should follow the standards of Section 508 (https://www.section508.gov) as well as those of W3C, the World Wide Web Consortium (https://www.w3.org), to ensure users with disabilities can access your materials.

Hardware and software needed to assist the differently abled should have been noted in your technology assessment, but if these were overlooked, you can always add them. Revisit the analysis of how technology is used in your library. Identify where assistive technology is currently located and where it should be added to help facilitate use. In addition to noting what adaptive technologies already exist in your library, look back at your demographic and user results to see what community needs are not being met.

Options

Depending on which unmet needs have been identified in your community, you may want to implement some of these simple and free solutions at your library.

- Screen readers. Screen readers read online websites and documents to the visually impaired user. With this ability to navigate websites, those who are visually impaired are able to be part of the online world. Two free screen readers are the ChromeVox screen reader (http://www.chromevox.com) and NonVisual Desktop Access or NVDA (https://www.nvaccess.org).
- Screen magnifiers. There are multiple options for screen magnifiers ranging from the integrated tools in Microsoft's operating system to more complex options for other systems. A list describing various magnifiers is available through the American Federation for the Blind (http://www.afb.org).

- Voice recognition software. Those who are unable to utilize a mouse or keyboard will be able to access online resources by enabling computers' native virtual assistants (Cortana, Siri, and Alexa, for example) or by adding speech-recognition software like Dragon Naturally Speaking.
- Ergonomic mice and keyboards. These devices are especially useful in communities with senior populations who want more online access.
- Closed captioning on embedded media. If your website includes embedded videos or audio recordings, having a closed-caption option can open doors for those with hearing difficulties.

Obtaining Accessibility Information from Vendors

As you add software and databases to your library's technology resources, it's a good idea to request vendor accessibility information. Ask your vendors to provide information describing how their products comply with 508 standards. This information can identify special accessibility features the product offers as well as areas of inaccessibility. One way to gather this information is a Vendor Accessibility Information Form. A sample template is available through the Section 508 Accessibility Program ("Voluntary Product Accessibility Template [VPAT]," https://www.section508.gov).

Resources

There are likely to be multiple agencies in your state, city, or community that are willing to create partnerships or provide resources related to adaptive technologies. For libraries just beginning to consider adaptive technology, I recommend the following readings.

- W3C, "Diversity of Web Users: How People with Disabilities Use the Web." The World Wide Web Consortium (W3C), an international community working to develop web standards, has explained various barriers to the web for those with different disabilities and how these barriers should be addressed (https://www.w3.org).
- New York Public Library, "Other Assistive Technologies" (https://goo.gl/HyPyFk). Although this web page by the New York Public Library has been archived and is no longer updated, it provides a great overview of disability resources that public libraries may offer. While all of these may not fit your needs, it is a good starting point to see how devices are used and implemented.
- Association of Specialized and Cooperative Library Agencies, Division of the American Library Association, "Assistive Technology: What You Need to Know Library Accessibility Tip Sheet 11" (https://goo.gl/yFJQXP). This American Library Association tip sheet describes tools

available to assist library users and lists overall tips for assisting users with disabilities.

MAKING A WORKABLE PLAN

In chapter 3, you created goals and outcomes. To reach those goals, you need to devise a workable plan for implementation. This plan will provide the action steps you'll take to reach these goals and achieve the desired outcomes. The action steps will help you determine a schedule, a budget, and a plan for implementation. Without an implementation plan, those lofty goals will likely remain unrealized.

Timeline

Creating a functional timeline will help you decide the sequence in which implementation and purchasing should occur. A timeline will lead your staff through a logical implementation process and will help to keep surprises to a minimum. Review your technology plan goals to determine what needs to happen when and in what order. You may find that it makes sense to start with two main areas: preparing the library's infrastructure and picking the "low-hanging fruit," the easy-to-implement items on your prioritized list. Let's examine this further.

The first step is looking at the infrastructure of your library's technology, the back end that supports the rest of the system. This infrastructure includes electrical service, bandwidth, routers, network connections, Internet, and security.

As a second step, after ensuring an adequate infrastructure, consider tackling any priority items that will be easy to implement—the so-called low-hanging fruit—early in the process. For example, one such task might be updating the staff PC in the children's room with antivirus software and Windows 10. Tasks like these often involve little to no cost, and the benefits can be seen immediately. Early success can build momentum for completing your plan. Concurrently with these easy steps, you might also start some large-scale projects such as building a makerspace area or creating a small business center. Projects like these usually have multiple components and can take a lot longer to complete.

In developing a timeline, be sure to schedule sufficient time for outside vendors as well as designated staff time to complete each task. Also, allow adequate time for any needed training of staff. On your timeline, be sure to include time for planning and evaluating each of these areas, not just for implementing the changes. Other considerations in timeline development include the following:

- Seasonal programming. Does the library schedule seasonal programming that should be avoided when planning changes in technology? For example, upgrading and changing out computers in the children's room in the midst of summer reading activities would not engender good feelings with the public or staff. A better approach would be to schedule technology changes to occur either before or after this busy season. Similarly, at an academic institution, avoid major technology implementations at the beginning of a semester or during finals.
- Dependent purchases. Are there some purchases that should be deferred until other items are in place? For example, it makes sense to wait for computers to arrive before purchasing subscription software.
- Funding considerations. When implementing a complex, multiyear plan, it may be necessary to spread out large expenditures over multiple years. Conversely, if grant money is used for a project, there may be stipulations regarding the time frame when the money must be spent. In some cases, grant-related purchases must be made within specific time periods (i.e., they cannot be made before a specified date or must be made before a specific deadline) or it may be necessary to acquire items early in the grant cycle so you can report usage statistics to the funder.
- Workflow. When scheduling implementation of the technology plan, include staff from each department affected by the changes. This will ensure a smoother transition with minimal impact to each department's work flow and daily services.

Locating Technology within the Library

Space constraints can become a challenge when bringing in new technology. "Where?" decisions about the location of equipment can determine the ultimate success or failure of a new technology project. The best resources will not be used if they are in the wrong department, hidden within a department, or placed in a hard-to-use location. As you consider the placement of technology, keep in mind the following:

- Who is your target audience? A computer with specialized software intended for use by entrepreneurs should be located in adult services. On the other hand, computers or technology designed to assist youth with learning about science, technology, engineering, the arts, and mathematics (STEAM) would be more useful in a youth or teen services area.
- What noise level is expected? For example, a station for creating podcasts needs to be in a soundproofed or quiet area. If not, the users' recordings will be subpar while other library visitors will complain about the noise level.

- What foot traffic will the new technology generate? If you expect the area to be busy, consider placing it away from any "quiet" spaces.
- Will the technology lend itself to collaborative work? If yes, make sure the area has space for multiple people at a computer and lends itself to small-group discussions.
- Do you want to highlight the technology? For instance, if you're adding a 3-D printer, consider placing it on a service desk or in a centrally located public area to draw attention to it.
- How will people find it? What signage do you need, and where should it be placed to help users discover the technology?

Creating Space

Finding space is a challenge for many libraries. You may be thinking, "Our library is out of space! We can't add a new computer lab, small business center, or makerspace in our existing building! There is just no room." In order to add new technologies, you will need to look at the current layout with a fresh eye. Here are some questions to consider as you try to carve out space within your library.

- Is there anything that is no longer necessary? Perhaps there is space that was previously dedicated to a program or service that is no longer needed or used.
- Do you have extra storage or office space? While the idea of using such an area for a technology program seems completely out of the box, the amazingly successful Innovation Lab at St. Petersburg College in St. Petersburg, Florida, was built in an underutilized storage closet. Technology space doesn't always need to be large to succeed.
- Do you have any nooks? Many older buildings have nooks that were originally designed to house pay phones. These spaces can be transformed into podcast or digitization studios with just a desk, a computer, and some minor soundproofing.
- Can you condense or remove shelving ranges? At City Library, we found several sections of the nonfiction collection where weeding was needed. This justified shifting the stacks, making it possible to remove several ranges. By selecting strategic ranges, it became possible to open floor space to be used for new technologies.
- Can you create a glass room? While putting up walls may create barriers and take away from the flow of the library, adding glass rooms can allow for new areas to be added to a main floor while maintaining sight lines for security and supervision.

- Are moveable walls or furniture a possibility? Moveable walls, chairs, and tables make it possible to create a flexible space that can be used as a small business center, training center, or other related purposes.
- Can you start small? Remember that you don't have to have everything in place on the first day. A new technology area might be initiated by using rolling carts or moveable furniture, or it could be started in a study room. As usage of the new technology begins to grow, you will have more justification for additional space.
- Security. Does the new area require new security? For example, if you are using an old office or storage area, or even a nook behind the stacks, does your staff have a visible sight line to the area? Should the security be physical, such as two-way mirrors or physical locks on the equipment? Do you need to monitor the area through video surveillance cameras? If you add cameras, how will they be monitored? If there are doors, can they be locked? If so, will a key be required for access? In thinking creatively about space, you do not want to incur security risks. Anticipate where and when hardware is at risk of being stolen. Even more importantly, avoid designing places that can make users vulnerable or might allow illicit behavior.

Floor Plans

Floor plans are essential for determining what space modifications may be needed. A detailed floor plan should include marks indicating power connections and the locations of other technology. Laying out proposed space changes over the library's existing floor plan will bring all components together, allowing you to identify potential issues before making modifications. Using a floor plan can even help with a simple, straightforward project like adding a new bank of computers to more complex projects. It will ensure that the required space and connections are available and that there are no unforeseen obstacles. Sharing floor plans that show proposed technology additions with staff and users can help create awareness, build enthusiasm, and generate buy-in.

Creating a floor plan is a great way to think realistically through the many details involved in a technology project. Beach Library's proposed floor plan (figure 4.1) was created using SmartDraw (smartdraw.com), but numerous other software products are available for drawing floor plans. A creation lab for children in grades K–5 and a maker area for teens were two new features added to Beach Library's children and teen room. Space for both features was created by removing and shifting stacks.

DEVELOPING A BUDGET

As you determine the support needed for existing and new technologies, you will create a budget to estimate the overall cost of the project. Without a fairly accurate budget, you really can't move forward. Without a budget, your plan is only an aspiration, not a workable instrument for achieving your goals.

To create the budget, it's sufficient to work with estimates rather than exact costs. For example, if you priced a computer for $278.74, put it in the budget for $300. It is easier to deal with round numbers. Also, make the estimate slightly higher than the actual costs you identified. Estimating higher will help you cover any unexpected costs such as possible price increases between the time the budget was prepared and the actual time of purchase. Finally, if you collect bids from contractors, make sure the bid will still be valid at the time you plan to make the purchase.

Identifying Onetime Expenses versus Ongoing Expenses

As you create a budget for the technology plan, make sure to track both onetime expenses and ongoing costs. Onetime expenses include initial expenditures that will not need to be replicated for several years; examples include hardware, some software, construction and other building modifications, furniture, electrical modifications, and signage costs.

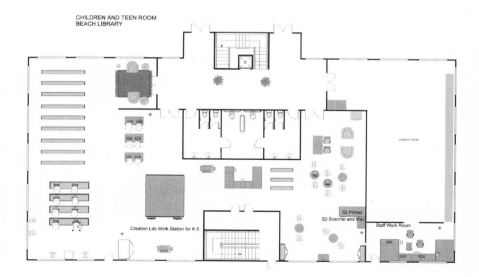

Figure 4.1.   Floor plan of proposed children and teen room technology

It's equally important to be cognizant of ongoing expenses, those costs that will recur each year. Make sure that either these can be absorbed into your current budget or future funds can be committed to cover them. Possible ongoing expenses to track include the following:

- SaaS (software as a service). These software products have an associated monthly or annual fee. Examples of SaaS include Microsoft Office 365 and the Adobe Creative Suite. Fees may be charged monthly or annually for these software packages.
- Staff. Does offering the new technology mean adding more staff? This may involve hiring more people to be able to extend hours or to add a service point. Successful implementation of many new technologies and technology training programs require staff with particular knowledge or abilities; it is vital to understand the skills needed for these positions. Adding staff could also include recruiting someone with specialized skills or arranging for specialized training for existing staff. In all cases, the budget for these positions needs to be sustainable.
- Outside consultants/experts. Although hiring a consultant is often viewed as a onetime expense, it could also be an ongoing cost. Examples might include outsourcing day-to-day management; emergency or after-hours support by a local technical company; and ongoing training provided by an outside organization.
- Internet. With additional technology and increasing user demand, your library might need to upgrade its bandwidth, requiring greater annual expenditures.

Associated Costs

Beyond the basic price of a technology device are additional costs that must be factored into your technology budget. Examples of these costs are expenditures previously identified within this chapter. These include furniture, building modifications and other infrastructure enhancements, installation and training, and staff. Neglecting to plan for these additional costs can lead to unforeseen expenses and could mean you're unable to properly implement your technology plan.

Furniture

When budgeting for technology, be sure to factor in the cost of furniture. Without appropriate furniture, new technologies may be underutilized. For example, without an appropriate and conveniently located printer stand, it may not be possible to place that new, large printer in an area where users can access it easily. An existing table used to support a newer, heavier printer can collapse if the table was not designed to withstand the weight.

New computer areas might need additional tables and chairs while a completely renovated area might need all-new furniture to fit the needs of its users.

Building Modifications: Construction and Infrastructure

Do walls need to be built to carve out a space for new technology or taken down to open up an area? Construction changes may be needed to convert a former staff workroom into part of a public area. Will an area be created with glass or walls to provide a new space for technology? Does an area need soundproofing because of the noise potential of equipment to be added? Soundproofing should be considered for small business meeting areas, collaboration hotspots, or areas used for video/sound recording or editing.

Take a good look at the library's electrical service as well. When upgrading technology or considering a location for new technology, evaluate the need for additional electrical outlets, drops, and floor outlets. Dedicated circuits and surge protection are also important considerations.

Do you need additional outlets or an overall upgrade? Does the building have adequate electrical service? What about lightning arrestors, building-level surge suppression, and location-specific surge protectors?

Are the library's networks properly set up and secured for appropriate staff and public access? Before you start adding more devices, make sure what you have (and plan to keep) are in line. Do your current routers need to be upgraded or replaced? Address this before adding a lot of new technology that must be configured and connected to the existing router. Failing to take care of this first might require staff to configure the router twice or could lead to unexpected technical issues.

For equipment requiring Internet access, review the overall Internet access to the area. Does the new technology need to be hardwired? Do you need an Ethernet connection in the space where the equipment will be located? Is the existing bandwidth sufficient to meet the new demand if you implement everything you've planned, or will bandwidth need to be increased? Will the new technologies require additional bandwidth, necessitating an increase in the library's overall bandwidth? Does the location have a strong Wi-Fi signal, or will you need to look at boosters or even hardwiring the area for adequate connectivity? Do you need additional network drops?

Securing your library's networks is vital. Before beginning to add any new equipment, make sure that networks are secure and that all existing technology is set up correctly. Otherwise, you could end up with security gaps created by the older technology.

Textbox 4.1. Key to Success

The key to success is to ensure the technology has the infrastructure to thrive.

Installation

Will installation and related tasks be accomplished by in-house staff or by outside vendors? There are costs associated with having an outside vendor install and set up the machines, but some libraries might prefer this option if the staff is limited in either time or expertise. Does your staff have the time to dedicate to installation tasks while also carrying out their daily duties? Do they have the necessary know-how to properly set up new technology? Third-party vendors might also be considered for initial staff and user training.

Do book stacks need to be shifted to accommodate the new technology? If so, professional movers might be needed to relocate shelving ranges.

Staff

Will implementing the new technology require additional staff? For example, if you are purchasing equipment for a new makerspace, do you plan to have existing staff work the makerspace area from an existing service point or from a new service point? Do you plan to limit the hours the new technology is available or to provide access whenever the library is open to the public? Are there enough qualified employees on staff already to cover a new service point, or are additional staff members needed? If more are needed, how many? If you plan to have the space run by staff with volunteer assistance or run entirely by volunteers, how will you vet those volunteers? How will you ensure they have the required skills and can commit the hours needed?

While it may not be a "cost" on the budget line, staff time is a resource that must be managed. It is important to understand how much time staff will be expected to work on this particular project and how doing so will fit into their daily schedules, both during the initial installation and training and then on an ongoing basis. For example, setting up a computer bank takes time— time to "load" the computers with the appropriate software, to install peripherals like printers and scanners, and to physically set up the area. Regular duties may need to be delayed or put on hold. If this can't be done, implementation may be substantially slowed or it may be necessary to hire a consultant or other outside help.

Additional Costs

Have you accounted for all additional costs for the area or technology to be added? Be sure to estimate costs accurately and to include the cost of any specialized training or extended warranties. These additional costs must be considered for your plan to be accurate. Construction and furniture costs can often be more expensive than the actual hardware and software to be purchased. For example, at Beach Library we created a proposal for a makerspace. The cost of hardware and software was estimated as $4,555, but the estimates for the related furniture and construction came to $5,600 and $600 respectively. In addition, custom signage was budgeted at $3,000. These estimates were included in the proposal for technology improvements to be made in the teen and youth area of Beach Library; a copy of the proposal is online at goo.gl/c3vpXX.

FUNDING

New computers? New furniture? There's no room in my budget! If that is what you are thinking, it's time to consider out-of-the-box options for funding the new technology needed by the people your library serves.

The most obvious and straightforward source for money is your current primary funder—the library board, the city council, the county commission, or the school board. Creating a detailed plan and budget, with clearly defined outcomes and goals that are in sync with the larger organization's mission, can help create buy-in from your governing organization. Getting new technology into your library's standard annual budget is the best scenario, so it's important to understand the process for obtaining that additional funding. Make sure you have a realistic timeline that dovetails with your funder's budget calendar. Furthermore, it's essential to help stakeholders—especially those who decide your budget—understand why this is vital. Remember, as you ask for money from your main funders, you are also competing with other departments and organizations for limited funds. Do your funders understand why new computers in the children's room are vital to the community? Do they agree that local businesses would benefit from a small business center in the library? To support the goals and outcomes you created in chapter 3, you'll want to provide demographic and usage numbers in support of your plan.

Outside the Box: Alternative Funding Options

Grants

Grants can be a good solution for funding projects that cannot be covered in your library's regular budget. Especially useful for onetime expenses such as implementing new technology, grants can jump-start your technology improvements and bring your plan to life. Your library should have access to information about national, state, and local government grants as well as those funded by the private sector. Your state library agency may be able to advise you about resources specific to libraries. For those just starting with grants, the Foundation Center (http://foundationcenter.org) is an excellent resource.

Grants require time and resources, both in applying and in implementing. Writing grant proposals is an in-depth task that relies on organizational statistics and a well-thought-out plan. Most grantors focus on project outcomes and require regular reporting on how funds are spent as well as project updates and statistical analysis of how grant funds are used. Each requirement of a grant must be met to secure the funding, so make sure your library can manage the administrative requirements.

Those new to grants will find a multitude of places to look for funding. As you explore grants, pay close attention to the following:

- Funders' primary mission. As an example, if the organization offering the grant is primarily focused on children, your grant should focus on children as well.
- Grant restrictions. Grantors are usually clear as to what they will and will not pay for. For example, some prohibit expenditures for marketing or limit the amount of money that can be used for staffing. Before you apply, make sure the grant requirements are in line with your needs and plans.
- Grant requirements. Is the grant aimed at a special population or need? For example, if you want to develop projects reaching local entrepreneurs or seniors, make sure the grant's requirements align with your target population.
- Budget. Each grant has parameters on how much money can be awarded and how the budget should be categorized. Before submitting your application, work out your entire budget so you can accurately state how the money will be used. Often grants do not allow much budgetary leeway. The monies awarded must be spent on items as presented in the proposal and approved by the grantor. Some grants also require "matching" funds from local sources to supplement the amount awarded.
- Timeline. Grant money must be spent within a specific period as determined by the grantor. Therefore, before applying, you must secure ap-

provals for the project from your library administration and select the vendors to be used so that the project can be implemented within the specific time frame.

Community and Strategic Partnerships

A partnership is a joint endeavor with another organization. Partnerships may be primarily financial, but they can also bring additional in-kind resources. The culture of collaboration is growing, and strategic partnerships with other organizations in your community can bring new services to library users in a cost-effective manner.

Libraries can partner with local nonprofits, with technology companies, and even with other government agencies. A successful partnership is mutually beneficial. The key to successful partnering is to have discussions on how the partnership will work—what each party brings to the partnership. The respective roles and responsibilities of both partners should be documented in a formal agreement or contract so that everything is clear and there are no misconceptions.

Partnerships may be on a large scale such as sharing space or they can be smaller, as in bringing in expertise for assistance or training. One example is partnering with the Small Business Administration to establish a makerspace to help entrepreneurs develop their businesses. A local college might offer staffing or computer assistance, or a local company might provide new equipment for a job training lab.

Before entering into a partnership agreement, ask yourself these questions.

- What is the overall benefit of the partnership to each partner?
- What is the library expected to contribute, and what can it expect in return from the partnering organization?
- What is the library's role?
- Is the partner contributing enough to justify the partnership?
- Which individuals will be the points of contact for each organization, and what are their responsibilities?
- Is the partnering institution reliable?
- How long will the partnership continue, and is it renewable?
- At the end of the partnership, what happens to any equipment provided by a partner?

Crowdsourcing

Beyond partnerships, your library can look to the community for funding through crowdsourcing for onetime expenses. GoFundMe, Donors Choose, and similar sites allow you to set up a donation drive for a specific project.

Using these sites makes it simple to set up and launch your campaign—but success requires planning. Here are some tips for a successful campaign.

- Demonstrate that the project is well thought out, with a budget and time-line.
- Focus on how the project will benefit users. Donors want to know that a project will significantly impact the community. For example, avoid a statement like, "The library needs a new computer lab because our computers are woefully out of date." Instead, focus on the purpose for which the new computers are needed—to provide job training, homework assistance, or whatever the desired outcome may be.
- With crowdfunding sites, simply creating the campaign is not enough. You also need to create a marketing plan to bring attention to the campaign, especially within your local community.
- Remember to acknowledge and provide a symbolic thank you to your donors. The expression of thanks should correspond to the donation size: smaller donations may be a recognized with a small token while large donations should be acknowledged with naming rights or recognition in a more elaborate way.

FINAL THOUGHTS

A well-designed plan that considers feedback from the public and the staff is vital in planning for technology. Implementing a plan that simply indicates "new computer" as an item to be acquired actually means selecting, purchasing, and installing a specific make and model within a given time frame. If you have only a vague notion about adding a makerspace, a center for teaching English as a second language, or a podcasting station but lack an understanding of all the associated costs, you can count on failure. A realistic plan that reflects a concrete budget and an understanding of associated costs is necessary for success.

Chapter Five

Writing Your Technology Plan and Getting It Approved

As has often been said, a plan in your head is not a plan—it's just an idea. Shaping your technology plan into a useful written document is fundamental to the success of the plan itself. By working through the first chapters of this book, you have created various components of your plan; putting everything together into one written document will help you articulate the plan and prepare you to move forward.

This chapter will lay out guidelines and tips for creating a coherent plan that will allow you to succeed. Different approaches are suggested, but the specific format for the written plan is up to you and will be influenced by the culture of your institution.

METHODOLOGY

Why should a plan be in written form? The value of a written technology plan is that it helps funders and other decision makers as well as staff members, users, and the community at large understand the direction the library is taking and why. This document serves as a roadmap for changes to come and should include the reasoning behind each technology goal. As a roadmap, it should be understandable and sufficiently detailed so that future developments, such as staffing changes, will not derail the plan.

The written plan is a summary of all the tasks completed so far and that will be completed in the later chapters of this book. These include the following:

• Technology assessment

- Community input and the definitions of options
- Goals and outcomes
- Planning
- Budgeting
- Criteria for evaluation
- Planning for the future

Each of these elements should be incorporated into the final written plan. The data gathered at each step—assessing existing technology, evaluating community and staff needs, soliciting feedback from the community, gathering budget information, and so forth—should be used to inform the written plan but need not be included in detail. For the most part, each topic will be addressed at an "executive summary" level, providing evidence of the foundation work that has been done but omitting the many details that have gone into developing the plan.

The document needs to have a single, unified message. While different members of the planning committee may work on different parts of the plan, the final document needs to have a coherent voice. To achieve this, it's often easier if one person takes the pieces of the plan and writes a draft of the entire document. Then members of the planning committee can review and edit drafts before the document goes outside the committee for further review by others.

The individual who undertakes this task should have strong writing skills, should understand the technology discussed, and most importantly, should be able to explain the technology in lay terms understandable by the general public. Even though this document is focused on technology, the intended audience must be kept in mind. This audience includes the library staff, library users, the community at large, and the library's stakeholders. It's important that the document be written clearly and not ladened with library lingo and tech-speak.

FOUNDATIONS FOR A GOOD TECHNOLOGY PLAN

The focus of your technology plan should be its goals and outcomes (see chapter 3). Both short- and long-term goals should be included, along with an overview of the entire planning process and the time frame for implementation. In addition, the plan should address how it is to be reviewed as well as when it is to be updated or when a new planning process is to be conducted; this will be discussed in more detail in chapter 10.

An effective written plan is direct and to the point. Think of the written document as a painting of a forest as a whole, not explicitly detailed sketches of individual trees. Although all the supporting documentation collected up to now will be useful to the staff when implementing the plan, highly specific information does not need to be included at this point.

Introduction

An effective way to begin the written plan is by citing the library's mission. This statement puts the technology plan in context and ties it to both the library's role and its broader strategic plan in a concrete way.

The best way to begin a discussion of the technology changes to be recommended is with an overview of the process that was used to develop the plan. The data that has been collected— including community needs and desires along with the assessment of existing technology and research conducted on new options—all serves as the foundation for the written plan. Describing the planning process and providing a brief history of the preparatory work already done helps build credibility for the final plan. Explaining the planning process and the research that's been done will make it clear why the plan was developed and why it is significant.

It's often useful to include basic demographic information about the library's service area to help the reader understand the future challenges the plan will address. In addition, you may want to include a summary of the community input you've collected, briefly describing how information was collected from those the library serves along with overall takeaways from the data collected. Explaining current and future community needs helps build a strong case for the technology that is being proposed to meet those needs.

Finally, include a list of the people who served on the planning committee and identify their official roles. It's important to give them credit for their hard work and to encourage public acknowledgment. Naming those who worked on the project can also help with buy-in from other staff members. It's evidence of how many people worked on the technology plan and proof that the plan did not just appear as one person's dream.

Focus on Goals and Outcomes

The primary focus of your written technology plan should be the goals and outcomes developed in chapter 3. State each goal along with related outcomes—the results to be realized as activities are conducted in support of the goal. The activities may include, in general terms, the type of technology to be acquired or training to be provided. While specific technology equipment has been determined and a budget created to cover the cost, remember that a high degree of detail is not needed at this point. The written plan is intended to be a summary of the process and should stick to the bigger picture.

Here's an example of a typical outcome: *Replace 40 percent of the public access computers with newer equipment*. This is an appropriate statement to include in the written, published plan. Note that this outcome does not specify that each public access station is to be upgraded with an HP 20 All-in-One AIO 19.5" HD+ Display desktop computer with Intel Dual Core Celeron 1.6GHz CP and 4GB DDR3 memory. While you may intend to purchase this particular device and may have included these specifications in preparing a budget, circumstances can change. The budget may prove to be more limited than you had anticipated. By the time you're ready to make a purchase this particular model may be no longer available. Perhaps a different computer model—one with better features—will have come on the market. Listing too much detail in your written plan can be limiting, unnecessarily restricting your options for making the best decisions in the future.

In addition to explaining the *what*—the goals, outcomes, and anticipated new technologies—the written plan should include a general timeline and criteria for evaluating the technology changes that are proposed.

Timeline

The timeline identifies the period of time covered by the technology plan and states the dates covered. Specifying the dates covered by the plan will help keep activities on track. It also serves as a reminder to keep the plan updated.

The time frame for each goal and objective should be identified too. In preparing the timeline, consider how long each activity will take. Consider also what needs to be done each year of the plan. Include new activities as well as ongoing tasks. In chapter 6 we will discuss how to properly determine a timeline, but remember to be realistic in your planning. Updating computers may be successfully accomplished within six months, but creating a new makerspace cannot be implemented in so short a period, especially if construction is involved.

Evaluating the Plan

The plan should also include the methodologies to be used for an ongoing evaluation of these new technologies. It's important to describe the criteria by which the library staff, funders, and the community will know whether specific initiatives have been successful. This is achieved through a solid evaluation plan, one that is also reflected in the timeline. Chapter 9 will explore evaluation planning in depth.

Formatting Your Written Plan

Before beginning to write the plan, determine whether your library, local government, or parent institution has a preferred format for such documents. They may even have a template for this purpose. There is no point in "reinventing the wheel" or creating a situation where you may need to revise the work if the format is rejected.

There are multiple ways to combine all this diverse information into a coherent plan. Regardless of the approach, remember to include all of the content listed in the "Methodology" section earlier in this chapter.

One approach to organization is to structure the plan around the individual goals and objectives. Another way is to focus on the outcomes. For instance, you may have a goal such as, *Provide support to Unity Library's small business community.* This goal would have arisen from the underlying research you conducted, research that identified the business community's need for collaborative workspace and marketing software. If you choose to focus on outcomes, you might list the various outcomes and then relate them back to the goals they serve. For example, your outcomes may be to *update and replace 40 percent of public computers* and *create a small business resource center.* These outcomes support larger goals and may help achieve multiple goals you've identified. One technology plan that uses this methodology is that of Boston University (explored below). By identifying those specific needs in the written plan, the *why* behind the goal will be clear to funders, your community, and your staff. For example, you may state that the library will buy Adobe software to support the community's needs, will develop a small business collaboration center, or will pursue other specific technology-related strategies. Indicate when the new resources will be available (e.g., Spring 20XX or First Quarter 20XX), keeping in mind the library's funding schedule and plans for implementation.

A third approach is to focus on the overall needs of the community. With community needs as the focus, the user surveys, feedback, and demographic information you've gathered will help build a case for new technology. You might state a community need and then identify the technology goals intended to address this need. For example, your assessment of the community and its demographics may have identified one or more of the following community needs: a lack of STEAM education for a growing youth population; insufficient workforce training that reflects the demand for changing job skills; or resources for an aging population. The goals and outcomes that the library will provide to meet these needs will range from updated computers and software, to programming, and to new, specialized hardware.

A final approach to organizing the plan might be to stress the library's current technology inventory and how demands for technology are expected to change. This approach might best fit the needs of a library that is not anticipating any major technology initiatives but instead is focusing on modernizing and expanding the technology already on hand.

Examples of Effective Technology Plans

Multiple examples of library technology plans may be found on the web. Although the content of each is very specific to an individual library, these examples provide ideas for content to include as well as for formats that can be emulated or customized to meet your needs.

The library's size should not determine how information is displayed in the plan. The choice of display or layout should be based on the content to be included and on the focus of the plan. If you are not constrained by a template or format from your governing institution and find yourself staring at a blank piece of paper, determining an effective format can be difficult. Luckily, inspiration for formatting is available online in the form of a number of good technology plans.

Listed here are technology plans that are particularly good at conveying the primary focus of their plan. Each plan has a very different style even though most of the information we've discussed is present in some form. A list of the plans along with the URLs where they may be found is provided at the end of this section.

- Boston Public Library. The Boston Public Library is one of the largest public libraries in the United States. Its plan covers a three-year period and looks at the technology of all twenty-five locations plus the Metro Boston Library Network. The plan focuses on the technology goals and outcomes and how they relate to the overall mission of the library. Each major goal is subdivided into outcomes that have specific activities associated with them. The arrangement of the plan allows for an easy assessment of its successes and failures. While the plan explains the new technological enhancements, it adheres to the concept of avoiding too much detail. This plan also includes a section on how it is to be implemented. By placing the plan on its website, the library has publicly committed to its success.
- Boston University. One of the top private colleges in the country, Boston University has approximately eight thousand students. Its library system consists of the main Mugar Library and several smaller, specialized libraries on campus. Boston University's technology plan is posted on an extremely visual website. The plan begins with a summary followed by core competency areas that were defined within the library's strategic plan. Each initiative is then color-coded to reflect how it relates to the strategic plan. This simple summary is followed by details of the planning process, including the community assessment, trendcasting, the overall planning process, and the assessment plan.
- Buffalo and Erie County Public Library. This is a well-structured plan for a large public library system comprised of a central library, eight city branch libraries, a bookmobile, and twenty-two contracting member li-

braries. The plan includes both a summary of the technology assessment and a description of the role of the system's technology support staff. This plan starts with an overall picture of the system's technology and then delves into specific projects (strategies) selected to achieve specific goals.

- Indiana State Library. The State Library of Indiana created a technology plan template for Indiana libraries to use. If your library, school, or local government doesn't have a preapproved format, this downloadable document can help you incorporate your technology specifics into an easy-to-use, workable document. The template, available in the appendix of this book, can guide you in fleshing out the content. Sample tables are also included and can help make information easily understandable to readers.
- Jackson County (Indiana) Public Library. Jackson County Public Library takes a completely different approach to the technology plan developed for its three library locations. Its plan is notable for its detail and level of transparency to the public and is one of the more detailed plans available online. The plan is not a static document but instead is posted on a web page, a feature that enhances its accessibility. It includes tables listing current and proposed items of technology. Goals and objectives are also included, along with training initiatives, an easy-to-understand timeline, budget details, and an evaluation schedule.
- Moultonborough (New Hampshire) Public Library. The Moultonborough Public Library serves the town of Moultonborough from a single location. The library's technology plan summarizes community needs that were identified by soliciting public input from four specific groups: adults, high school students, the class of 2024 (young students), and businesses. The plan explains the library's goals and, for perspective, includes a visual map of the current technology. The additional inclusion of a proposed visual map of the final plan would have been a welcome addition, but the overall structure of the technology plan as presented is highly effective.

Each of these plans is available online for viewing. Review them and analyze the format of each to determine whether one of these approaches will work for displaying the information you want to emphasize with your staff, community, and stakeholders.

- Boston Public Library, "Technology Plan," 2013–2016, http://bpl.org/general/trustees/BPLtechplan2013-2016.pdf
- Boston University, "Boston University Technology Plan," FY 2015–2020, http://bu.edu/tech/plan
- Buffalo and Erie County Public Library, "Technology Plan," 2017–2021, https://goo.gl/6NcXdz
- Indiana State Library, "Indiana Public Library Technology Plan Template," http://cc.readytalk.com/cc/download/schedule/jtecl3xh0ywf

- Jackson County (Indiana) Public Library, "Technology Plan," 2015–2017, http://myjclibrary.org/technology-plan
- Moultonborough (New Hampshire) Public Library, "MPL Technology Plan," 2017–2018, https://goo.gl/ueMnEp

As you can see from the variety represented in these plans, there is no one "right" format. Decide what components you want to stress—the planning, the community needs, the goals, the timeline, or the outcomes. The key to a successful document is making it easily understandable and readable by everyone, especially by those who are not familiar with the library's technology planning process.

Notice that some plans were in PDF while others used a web-based layout with one or more dedicated pages on the library's website. Either method is appropriate for posting to the web. A PDF document can be easily created from a word processing document for uploading to your website. This is probably the easiest, quickest, and most efficient way to share your plan in a digital environment. Its disadvantage is that it cannot be revised and users need specialized software (commonly available but still specialized) to read the document. Because a PDF document cannot be altered, this format is preferred to a document in Word or other word processing programs.

A second method for sharing your plan involves adding a page to your website where the plan is displayed. Updates can be added to this page as projects are completed, creating a more dynamic presence for your plan. A web page is often preferable because it's considered more user-friendly and easier to access from the Americans with Disabilities Act and user-experience perspectives. However, this approach requires the ability of a staff member who can move the content from a word processing document to an HTML web page.

GETTING THE PLAN APPROVED

Simply writing a technology plan does not guarantee that the plan will come to fruition. In order to have your plan succeed, you need approval from funders and administrators as well as a realistic budget. If you have kept these decision makers informed about community needs and the library's plans, they will be more receptive to your request. Look for opportunities to talk with key individuals and constituent groups in terms of aspects of the plan that may be of special interest or importance to them. Explain to these groups—and to those who are connected to them—how they may benefit from the proposed technology.

As you work to get approval, understand the financial deadlines of your governing organization. Find out key dates in the budget year, and note when requests must be submitted. It's often necessary to apply for large budget expenses more than a year in advance, so plan your timeline accordingly.

If sufficient funds are not available from your primary funding source, you may decide to pursue grants or partnerships as ways to implement the technology your community needs. Before grants or partnerships are developed, though, the plan needs to have buy-in and approval from those who govern and administer the library.

USING THE PLAN TO REACH GOALS

Your plan should be transparent. This means that all stakeholders—the staff, funders, library users, Friends of the Library, and community groups—should have easy access to the plan. The technology plan, or at least a version of the plan, should be available to the public. Posting the plan on the library's website is often a good solution. Many libraries post an early draft for public review and solicit feedback. Once the plan is adopted, it's posted in its final, approved format. The final version should include the name of the governing body that granted the approval and the date the plan was accepted. Publicizing this information both shows the governing body's support for the library's technology activities and keeps the library accountable for implementing the plan within the designated time frame.

FINAL THOUGHTS

No matter the format you choose, it is important to put your plan in writing. The written plan is the overall outline of what you intend to accomplish regarding technology and of why these activities have been selected. Without a written plan, all the work you've done will remain fragmented and will not come together to accomplish the intended goals. Having a strong, well-written plan is a prime predictor of success. Without it, your ambitions and goals for the library's technology are likely to fall to the wayside due to staffing changes or just the everyday tasks that overwhelm us in our libraries.

Chapter Six

Successful Implementation

By working through the previous chapters, you have created a complex plan with goals and outcomes as well as a roadmap for achieving those goals. Even with the best directions, though, we can fail to reach our destination if we do not successfully implement our plans. In this chapter, we will look at tactics and best practices to ensure successful implementation so that your library's technology services will thrive.

Key areas on which to focus for success are project management, communication about the progress of implementation, and training. Basic project management strategies are essential to guide the project from beginning to end—without them, the best-laid plans can fail. Communication is a vital part of a strong implementation plan with staff, community members, and stakeholder groups; all need to be informed about developments in implementation and about the details of the new technology. Without training, the new technologies will not be used to advantage. Both project management and communication will be discussed here while training will be addressed in chapter 7.

PROJECT MANAGEMENT

Project management involves guiding a multiphase task from start to finish with the goal of completing it on time and within the approved budget. It can be a difficult skill to master, especially while juggling other job responsibilities. This chapter assumes that one individual has been tapped as the project manager to lead implementation, either for the whole plan or for a specific outcome within the plan. The best practices discussed here will help those without much previous experience in this type of management who become "accidental" project managers.

In this chapter, we'll focus on how to lay out the implementation of a specific technology in an organized fashion. This will help you identify potential red flags—conflicts and risks that need to be addressed carefully before they become crises.

Creating an organizational system will help you stay focused. It will also equip you with the information needed to explain to other staff and users why a particular task needs to be done at a particular time. It will prepare you to answer questions such as these: When new hardware arrives, will you have time designated to set it up? If you will need help from an outside contractor or volunteers, will they be available when needed? What impact will this project have on your normal workload and that of others? Will services to library users be affected? All of these questions need to be answered in advance and the answers communicated to everyone involved. Without this level of planning, construction can be delayed or newly purchased hardware may be left sitting in boxes in the back of the library.

Before jumping into your implementation, take the time to organize your project around three points: objectives, timeline, and staff.

Objectives

Moving from the theoretical plan to actually making changes in the real world can be daunting, but a strong plan with defined outcomes can help bring your vision to reality. Each of the technology plan's objectives may actually be a project in itself, so examine all of them with a project management eye.

The objectives of implementation should be already clearly defined in the written, approved technology plan. As you have worked through this book, you identified the specific resources necessary to implement the equipment or services to be added. By now, funds have been allocated and space to house the project has been identified. If you have not already done so, create a detailed list of tasks that must be done to complete each objective; these tasks should include those to be done in-house and those for which you must rely on outside help.

Timeline

The project's timeline—the schedule for completing tasks in sequence and on time—is your guide for success. The timeline will help you understand what needs to be done, when it needs to be completed, and whether everything is on track. For example, your approved technology plan may have this goal: *Launch makerspace, summer 20XX.* Although this item is stated in brief fashion in the plan, the timeline provides the specifics and the sequence of tasks that your coworkers, all stakeholders, and you need to keep in mind if these are to happen on schedule.

The timeline should lay out when each part of the project is to be carried out and should identify the date by when it is to be completed. This will clarify the order in which tasks need to be performed and will identify dependencies, those tasks that rely on other tasks to be completed first. For example, construction and remodeling projects require that walls are built before floors are placed and that electricians complete wiring before painters arrive. Organizing the sequence of events is like putting together a puzzle: all the puzzle pieces must be placed in the correct order.

The timeline should reflect all aspects of technology planning discussed in previous chapters. These include construction and infrastructure, purchasing, installation, and training. It may also be necessary to contract with third-party vendors for completing specific tasks and to coordinate with government agencies regarding permitting, inspections, and approvals; these activities should be reflected in the timeline too.

Major tasks should be divided into smaller steps, each with definite deadlines. Significant deadlines should be identified as milestones, those that must be met for the project to remain on schedule. The timeline should also indicate arrangements to keep staff, stakeholders, and the community informed about progress being made. It is the responsibility of the project manager to keep an eye on all these details as well as on the big picture, ensuring that deadlines are met and the project continues to move forward.

The Role of Staff in Project Implementation

Before beginning any implementation, have a clear understanding about those who will be working on it. Carefully define the role of the project manager and the roles of all who will be involved in the project (both staff and outside contractors) as well as roles of other library staff members who may be affected by the project.

For each task, describe precisely who is responsible for each component. For example, if the timeline lists tasks such as "Install electric outlets" or "Wi-Fi enabled for area," identify exactly who will be responsible for each activity—no matter how big or small—that's part of completing the task. Providing this level of information will avoid confusion and misunderstandings down the line.

At this point, unlike the big-picture approach recommended earlier for preparing the written plan, you need to anticipate specifics. For example, when identifying staff roles on the timeline, the level of detail should indicate particular individuals, not simply a department. The person to be assigned to carry out component activities should be identified as "Mary from IT" or "Steve from Children's." As the project manager, make sure these individuals and their supervisors understand what will be required from them, how much time will be needed, and when these tasks need to be completed.

Are You on Your Own?

For smaller projects, or in smaller libraries, you may not have a formal team helping you. Even so, it is recommended that you create a full timeline and use a project management approach. These tools help you keep in mind all the tasks that need to be accomplished and when they need to be completed. Working through the timeline and employing a task-management system will enable you to keep the project in the forefront, despite the pressure of other responsibilities.

Planning for Personnel

If your technology project involves reallocating staff or adding new duties to a current staff position, be sure to analyze the other responsibilities of these employees. Ensure there's adequate time for them to complete all assigned duties. In order for the staff to successfully manage the new technology, some responsibilities may need to be shifted away from their current position either temporarily or permanently. When adding job duties, make sure job descriptions are revised to list all new responsibilities. Similarly, any tasks that employees will no longer perform should be removed and the evaluation criteria should be revised so that job descriptions accurately reflect employees' work.

Are you hiring new staff? The logistics of bringing new people on board can take a great deal of time and effort, involving coordination with the human resources office or following your institution's hiring practices. You must define the position and determine its salary range. For highly technical positions or for jobs that involve working with specialized software, identify the skills required; they are likely to be different from those needed for existing positions.

Does the position require a library degree or training in a specialized technology? If you need to hire someone with skills or technical knowledge you do not have yourself, look for help in evaluating candidates. Those who work in technical fields elsewhere—either in your parent institution or for local businesses or organizations—may be willing to assist with evaluating applications and interviewing applicants. If you cannot find help within your institution or community, there are professional companies (recruiting and staffing agencies) that can assist with the hiring of specialists. While this may seem an unnecessary expense, hiring an ill-qualified person can cost even more in the long run.

In addition to determining a new employee's qualifications and salary, your project timeline must also take the budget process into consideration.

While it may be ideal to have a new employee come on board in the project's early planning stages, this may not be feasible. Funding for positions may not be available until a certain time, such as the beginning of a new fiscal year or the starting date of a grant.

Resources for Project Management

There are easy-to-use software tools available to keep you and your team organized. Project management software is an especially useful tool for large-scale implementations, ones that involve a lot of steps, changes, or many different people.

Two good, free software options are Trello (http://trello.com) and Zoho (https://www.zoho.com/projects). With both it's possible to assign tasks to individuals and to allow team members access to a single account where they can share documents and resources as well as collaborate.

Let's look at each of these tools more closely. With Trello, each implementation project can be divided into "boards." Within each board a series of decks can be created; each deck contains individual tasks. The tasks are given a due date and assigned to an individual. Each task can have its own checklist and be tagged and categorized so it can be found easily. Zoho is a more robust example of project management software. It allows you to create dependencies for specific tasks, deadlines, and overall lists of tasks. Project managers can also create milestones to ensure the project is running on schedule.

Beyond these specialized resources, a simple shared calendar or spreadsheet can be used to create an effective timeline for managing multiple aspects of a project. For shared documents, look to what your library currently uses. For example, Google Drive with Calendar or Microsoft Office with Outlook may already be familiar to your staff and may be sufficient for smaller projects.

COMMUNICATION

Communication, though often overlooked, is one of the most important factors in the success of a project. It is important to maintain communication with all key groups—the staff and other stakeholders as well as community members. This should not be reserved for the final stages of a project but should be an integral part of the entire process. Project managers need to ensure that information is shared about any setbacks that may delay the project as well as about milestones reached. The level of information needed by different audiences may vary, but all need to know about progress being made and whether any obstacles will cause the timeline to be adjusted.

When staff members, users, or stakeholders are left on their own to figure out what is going on, the result can be a lack of buy-in, general confusion, and—even worse—the circulation of misleading information. A new development, such as when the children's department will get new computers, should not be a mystery to anyone. Avoid situations where staff members can only shrug their shoulders in response to questions from library users. Transparency is important beginning with the earliest steps in developing a technology plan; it's even more vital during the implementation phase.

Communicating with Staff

How do you typically get news to staff members? Is this method effective? This is a question you need to ask yourself when planning for communication related to the technology plan. All staff members need to understand the plan in general terms and need to know the timeline and the goals of the project. Poor communication with the staff can lead to huge issues and might even undermine a project's success. If there are no official communications or project updates, the staff will still receive news through the grapevine or other unofficial channels.

Imagine that new computers have arrived. Some staff members will have seen the boxes being delivered. It's time for an official message such as, "The computers for the children's department have arrived. We're waiting for the electrician to come next week and install new outlets. Then the IT staff will install the computers. The project is behind schedule by about a week, but everything should be ready for students before school starts at the end of the month." Without a message like this, questions can easily arise, such as, Why are the computers sitting in boxes in the back? Will we be ready for our back-to-school open house on the third?

For an example of communication related to a more complex project, consider the installation of podcast stations. A podcast station consists of a computer with a good microphone or even multiple microphones and with software to record audio and to edit the audio recordings. Plans likely call for the station to be set up in a soundproof room (or a room that's as close to soundproof as you can manage in your library) and might include adding "soft furniture" to help absorb noise. The station may include additional software and hardware options for users: Skype with a Skype call recorder or other software to interview people remotely; a portable XLR recorder to record multiple audio inputs from multiple microphones; audio editing software like Audacity or Garageband; and additional software for editing, changing formats, and uploading software to a podcasting distribution site.

With the introduction of a podcast station, the staff will typically have many questions, such as, What can you do on a podcast station . . . and what the heck is a podcast? Why was this technology selected? How does it work?

Who will benefit from it? Where in the library will the stations be located? Why there? Who will be responsible for the stations? Can a podcasting station be used for other purposes such as creating oral histories, voice-overs for videos that users are creating, or for editing sound in general? Will I receive training related to this new service? If so, how and when?

If you do *not* provide the staff with this kind of information and fail to answer questions early in the project, rumors will start. Once misinformation starts spreading, it's difficult to correct. Frustration will rule the day—your own frustration as well as that of the staff. It may even extend to library administration and the public.

As soon as details about the new technologies are available, allow the staff to ask questions and gather information. In the stress of handling all the tasks involved in project implementation, it's easy to overlook the need for regular communication. Planning for it in advance will make sure it gets done.

So, how will you communicate? I recommend developing a communication plan that uses multiple channels to reach staff at different times and in different formats. A simplistic approach that proposes only that "once a week we will hold a staff meeting to update people on progress" is not realistic. Of course, it's a good idea to include updates in regular staff meetings, but that form of communication is not enough.

Communication channels can include—but aren't necessarily limited to—the following:

- Briefings provided to managers with information they can distribute to their departments
- Email blasts to all staff
- Staff-area signage that is updated regularly
- Postings to staff-only outlets such as blogs, Facebook groups, or intranet sites

Make sure all staff members are kept in the loop. This includes everyone from managers to part-time shelvers, full-time and part-time employees, maintenance and custodial staff, volunteers, and student workers. Why should all these individuals be regularly informed? Often, they are the ones who interact directly with library users; they're all seen by the public as representatives of the library. It's important for each of them to be able to respond positively when asked about the new technology.

As the launch date looms closer, the staff can be blindsided by questions if there has not been adequate communication. If they lack information about features of the new technology and how it will be used, staff members can feel as though they've been left in the dark. This may lead to negative attitudes. Staff members may be confused and anxious about their roles when changes are implemented. The result can be a negative emotional climate in which even the most carefully written policies and procedures don't succeed.

Communicating with Stakeholders

Stakeholders are people who are involved with the library and who are affected by its actions. Who are your library's stakeholders? They certainly include those who provide the budget and oversee the library. They also include the library's advisory board, the Friends of the Library organization, and members of the library foundation. Stakeholders include the library's governing body and may include other local government agencies as well as school officials. If the library is using grant funds to implement technology changes, be sure to include grantors among stakeholders who should be apprised of developments.

Stakeholders should not hear from you only when you are requesting funds. As part of a larger relationship-building process, provide them with regular updates and include them in ongoing communications about your projects. Stakeholders need to understand the impact of projects, how the library's goals—and the initiatives supporting those goals—will benefit library users, and why the success of this technology project is vital.

Stakeholders expect and deserve to be "in the know" about library matters. They need frequent updates, either at their regularly scheduled meetings or via email. It's important that they be kept informed so they can understand the changes that are being made and how these will benefit the community. For small achievements, email updates may be sufficient. For large-scale projects, you may want to provide more formal updates about progress. In addition to announcing when project milestones are met, inform stakeholders of any significant issues that may delay the project so they are not caught off guard by setbacks.

Some stakeholders, especially organizations or government agencies that provide grant funds, may require a specific reporting process. These organizations will outline when updates are due and what should be reported. Information on the project's status and on expenditures may be requested at defined intervals. Failing to meet reporting deadlines for grants may result in your library having to return or even forfeit grant money and can damage your reputation as a grant administrator. Don't miss these dates.

Communicating with the Community

Just as it's important to keep staff and stakeholders in the loop, it's also important to inform the public of changes, both before they happen and while they are underway. Tell library users and other community members in advance about changes, especially if they're likely to interrupt normal services.

It's simple courtesy to provide this information because it helps people avoid "wasted" trips to the library when they can't complete the purpose of their visit. Aim to supply information that heads off questions indicating frustration or anxiety, questions such as, What in the world is going on in the old microfiche room? Why is the wall in the children's room coming down? Why are all the computers missing from the computer lab? What do you mean "the lab is closed today"? My paper is due tomorrow!

In addition to helping library users plan their visits, regularly sharing updates and news about the project can help build buzz and excitement. The community is not a single, captive audience but a collection of many different groups of people. For this reason, it can be difficult to relay timely messages to everyone who needs an update. To inform as many people as possible, here are some approaches that have worked well for others and that may provide good places to start.

- Signage. The importance of effective signage cannot be overstated. Well in advance of actual changes, post signs about construction, the unavailability of equipment, and noise that may occur related to modifications. For maximum effect, signage should be posted in multiple locations. Locations to consider include the area or department where the change will occur, the circulation desk, and any messaging boards or dedicated announcement spaces you have within the library. The messages posted on signs inside the library should also be shared via the library website and social media.
- Word of mouth. Word of mouth is a highly effective means of communication. Promote it through interactions staff members have with the public each day. Staff members will inevitably relay information about changes in the library; be sure they're equipped to relay a message that's accurate and positive. Each interaction with a library user is an opportunity for a brief mention of upcoming events. Take advantage of other existing opportunities, such as public programs and planned outreach events, to announce updates. For example, the end of a story-time session provides an excellent opportunity to alert families to an upcoming change, whether it's a wall that will come down next week or the expected closing of the computer bank so new machines can be installed.
- Pictures tell the story. Users love to have a peek at the inner workings of the library. Use photos to document activities from demolition and construction to unboxing new equipment. The photos can be shared via email using your library's mailing lists and can be posted to social media and the library's website. Social media works best for photos of small unboxing moments (where a staff member opens a box and reveals the new technology). Use the website and email lists to publicize large-scale projects. Is a wall being demolished? Are old computers being removed from services?

These major visual moments can be of high interest. Make sure you document and share them. The images and videos can be used to create animated gifs, memes, and other viral media. You can even create programs around the events as well by using the old computers as part of an upcycling event or other art program.

- Community news. There are multiple channels within your community for news, both official and unofficial. These include newspapers and community groups on Facebook and other social media sites. Any major announcements should be posted to these forums. In the marketing section that follows, we will discuss formal press releases that can be used on these occasions.

PROMOTING NEW TECHNOLOGY WITH MARKETING

Creating a Marketing Plan

Beyond the timeline established for implementing a large-scale project, you also need a separate marketing plan. This plan may—and likely should—be managed by an individual or team other than the project manager, but both groups should work together so the marketing reflects the project timeline. As with project management, though, the responsibility for marketing often falls to a staff member without training or experience in this field.

How can you create a marketing plan to highlight a new technology service if you don't know anything about marketing? The first step is to look within your library and your governing institution for expertise. Your school, city, or county may have a marketing specialist you can use. If you're on your own, here are some basic tips for getting started.

Marketing your technology project actually begins with the early planning but then usually slows until the technology is closer to implementation. For news about major changes—such as a new makerspace area or job resource center—announce the project as it begins, giving its estimated opening date. For small-scale projects, it may not be necessary to announce the project's beginning stages.

To develop an effective marketing campaign, consider all of the components listed below. Create a multifaceted approach that will reach as many people as possible, as many times as possible, and with as little effort as possible. It is often said that people need to hear something three times to internalize it. Don't worry about saying something too many times. An individual may miss any one of these marketing touch points and will need other opportunities to become informed. A well-designed plan will have the same message, in different formats and maybe with different angles; each will help achieve the goal of getting the word out.

The more advance planning you invest in your marketing approach, the more effectively you can use your time in implementing it. Early planning pays big dividends and helps ensure no opportunity is missed. For example, if press releases are written and social media videos and graphics are prepared well before they're needed, they're more likely to be rolled out on schedule, even if unanticipated challenges occur.

Basics of Marketing

Developing a marketing strategy for your new technology blends in-house promotion, social media promotion, and other techniques for getting news out into the community. Address each of these areas to create a clear, coherent message that energizes users about your new technology.

With bigger or specialized projects, take time to properly brand the area. A brand helps with consistent verbiage on signage and in marketing. Create a meaningful name that will help users identify its purpose. The name may be as simple and straightforward as "Sound Stations" or "Podcasting Area" or could be more creative or catchy. The terminology will directly impact people's perceptions and can affect the use of the area, so think carefully when branding new areas. Effective names avoid library jargon or highly technical terms. It's possible that the name will be determined by the project's funding. If the area is made possible through a partnership, a grant, or a gift from a major donor, the library might provide naming rights, but this would have been stipulated when the funding was awarded.

Marketing to the Staff

The staff is a key group to include in marketing new technology. Without staff buy-in, it is hard to have a successful project. Staff members need to be aware of all specialized software within their location, not just their department. Depending on your library's size, the scope of internal marketing will vary. A small library may need some signs and discussion at department meetings, while medium and large libraries may need a formal plan.

Does a staff person at Beach Library need to know all the details about the new makerspace at the City Library? Probably not. But the Beach Library staff does need to know that there will be a makerspace at City Library, who can use it, and what can be done with it. In this way, the staff will be able to promote the makerspace to prospective users.

The best way to help someone understand new technology is to let them try it out. Training will be explored in detail in chapter 7, but even a brief orientation to new software or hardware can help the staff feel more comfortable about discussing it with users.

General suggestions for effective communication with the public apply to the staff as well. Marketing to the staff may be in the form of posters and signs in the staff area, email blasts, and discussions during staff meetings. With extended service days and six- and seven-day-a-week operations, the library staff works a variety of hours. It's especially important to include everyone, making sure no staff member is left out of the communication loop.

Visual Marketing

Before you begin developing marketing materials, make sure you understand any relevant guidelines set forth by your library system, local government, or institution. These guidelines may be specific as to acceptable fonts, templates, and colors. Your library or governing institution may have additional requirements regarding the acceptable use of logos and disclaimers that must be included. Learn all the requirements before you start to avoid redoing any marketing pieces.

For marketing programs with shoestring budgets, it may be necessary to create materials in-house. If you are designing your own materials, be sure to carefully consider fonts, colors, and the overall graphic design. Make sure there is high contrast between the font color and its background. Certain complex fonts and some color combinations can be hard to read, especially for people with color blindness. The website Colblindor is one of several offering a simulator that analyzes signage and marketing for color blindness issues ("Coblis: Color Blindness Simulary," http://www.color-blindness.com). To ensure your products are readable and deliver the message you want to promote, request feedback from those who are knowledgeable about your new technology area and from some people without prior information about the upcoming service.

Permanent Signage

Signs should deliver a clear message that helps users understand what is promoted and where it's located. Traditional signs signal distinct service areas and bring attention to them. Permanent signage should be large and easy to read, and able to grab the visitor's attention, but with aesthetics that are consistent with the rest of the library's interior.

Before ordering signage, consider what it needs to do. Who is the target audience? An appropriate sign appealing to children (and their parents) may need to be different from one intended for seniors. From how far away do users need to read the sign? When considering a sign's size, think about where it is to be placed and from what points it should be viewable. Should the sign be visible from the main entrance? Within the reference department?

Remember that a sign on a door is only visible to someone standing right in front of the door.

Posters

Posters are a tried-and-true method for bringing attention to services and resources available at the library. In-house displays can be a fun way to draw in users but must follow the library's policies and procedures. Strategically placed posters can supplement large exhibits by bringing extra attention to a new feature.

Posters can also be outreach tools, and their images can even be used digitally. Physical posters can be placed in community locations frequented by audiences for the new technology. Images can be sent as an email announcement and used on social media. Such methods not only promote the technology to existing users but also reach the larger community.

Even if you are not a designer, there are easy-to-use resources for creating posters based on templates. These are available within your library and on the web. They include Adobe and Microsoft Office, both of which are probably already installed on staff computers. Web-based tools for creating graphic designs include PosterMyWall (postermywall.com) and Canva (canva.com), to name a few.

Social Media and Email Marketing

Social media sites such as Facebook, Twitter, and Instagram already have your users' eyes, so it makes sense to focus some of your marketing energy on these media. While it is easy to post in social media, it's more difficult to post effectively. Here are some tips to help you succeed with social media marketing.

- Spread the word. Creating strong social media posts can help get the word out beyond your immediate followers. Ask other local organizations to share your posts about new technology with their followers. Promotional accounts of your city, county, or school system, as well as those of other relevant local groups, will reach a wider circle of potential users.
- Utilize hashtags. "Hashtag" is the term for the hashtag symbol # used at the end of a post in Twitter and Instagram. People use these to find information or similar posts. For example, using the hashtag #yourcityname (using the actual name of your city) will help local residents find your post just as #yourschool will reach students at your institution. By employing hashtags, you can promote resources to more people, potentially reaching everyone in your community.
- Schedule and plan. Scheduling posts may seem counterintuitive given the spontaneous feel of social media. To be effective, though, you need well-

thought-out messages that are posted at times when they will be seen by the most people. Messages that appear when viewers are offline are likely to be missed. Creating posts shouldn't be a daily activity. Instead, designate time to create messages that will be posted on specific days and at specific times of day. An effective schedule might be biweekly or even monthly. Regularly set aside time to create messages for all social media accounts. Consider using a commercial social media manager such as Buffer (buffer.com) or Hootsuite (hootsuite.com) to manage your social media; these allow you to schedule multiple posts on multiple platforms in a single place. In addition, these managers will help you find better hashtags and the best times to post to various social media. They also bring together replies, comments, likes, and other responses from social media to a single account. Spontaneous posting should be planned and carried out to promote events or highlight the technology in use. For example, if you know a teen group will be holding a maker program on Thursday at 3:00 p.m., think ahead about what pictures you want to capture so you don't miss something. Schedule time during the program to snap photos and post them instantly to social media. If a local business person is giving a talk to highlight the library's new job resource center, get pictures of the speaker alone and with the staff, audience members, and any stakeholders who attend the program. Post these to social media, and be sure to share them with stakeholder groups.

- Go visual—or better yet—go video. Text-based posts on social media have lower user engagement than do pictures or video. Pictures and visual posts are more effective than straight text, but video has the highest level of engagement. This trend is certain to continue. Consider creating short videos (under two minutes in length) that promote new technology.
- Email marketing. Updates by email can be another highly effective way to communicate with your users. Email marketing can be done with little or no budget. By using a service like MailChimp (Mailchimp.com), you can create a customized template to email people who previously signed up to receive announcements via the library's mailing list. As with social media, mailing lists can and should be used for more than just announcing new technology. This is an effective way to share information and show users what's new at the library.

Marketing to Your Community

Outreach activities to let the community know about new technology available at the library can take different forms, depending on what is being implemented and the population to be targeted. Community outreach may be achieved with a specialized flyer or poster that is distributed to specific groups or displayed where these groups congregate. Outreach could also be accomplished with a short talk to a social or civic organization. Other examples include the following:

- Presentation to the Chamber of Commerce that promotes the library's new small business area or new resources for entrepreneurs or job seekers
- Distribution of flyers through local schools, churches, or after-school programs to promote youth or teen makerspaces
- Contacts with local nonprofits or community groups via social media, email, or phone inviting their constituents to try out new technology at the library.

Other Methods

There is no one best way to promote a new technology center, and it's not possible to promote it too much, but it's important to promote it effectively. Depending on your users, the community, and the timing of the implementation, some techniques will be more effective than others. Here are additional ideas to bring attention to new technology-oriented services at your library.

- Kickoff event. Are you opening a new service or focusing on a new service area? A kickoff or grand opening can generate excitement and bring people to the library. This can be an especially good way to draw those who are not regular library users. Be sure to invite people from key demographic groups to attend the event. For example, for the grand opening of a small business resource center, encourage small business owners to attend. The local chamber of commerce and small business meet-up groups would also be important contacts to include. During the event, stakeholders can enjoy a moment of positive feedback from the public while community members interact with the new service, creating a good-will event where the library's services are at center stage.
- Press releases. Press releases provide an opportunity to tell your story in your own words. A release helps get the news out to the community through local newspapers, blogs, radio, and TV. Your library or local government should have a list of local news contacts. In addition, many major newspapers accept submissions of community events at no charge—make sure your events are included. If your parent organization (city, county, school system, or university) cannot assist with a press release, there are fee-based companies that can distribute these. While this might not be a worthwhile investment for every new promotion, it may have value when publicizing larger implementations. Some services, such as PR Newswire (prnewswire.com), offer discounts for nonprofits and schools, so the pricing can be reasonable.

- Word-of-mouth marketing (WOMM). Most libraries find that the single most effective way to promote new resources and services is through word-of-mouth marketing—and this begins with the staff. The basics of word-of-mouth marketing are simple. All staff members should be able to recite basic facts about a technology and its benefits and to answer frequently asked questions. Providing staff members with facts about a new service helps keep it in the forefront of their minds so they can mention it to users, even if the new service is not in their department or immediate location. For example, while assisting customers at the circulation desk, staff might inquire, "Will you be attending the makerspace opening next week? They will have sewing machines, a 3-D printer, and robots." Beyond this statement, the staff should be able to provide details on each technology named and how/why the user will want to use the technology.
- Targeting special populations. Beyond the generic marketing channels already described to reach the general public, take a step back and consider the target audience for the new technology. Who is the audience? How are they likely to consume news? How can you reach them? Who do you know who is in touch with them? Depending on the technology, you may decide to approach senior centers, preschools, scout groups, local job centers, or other groups who work with and are trusted by those you want to reach.

FINAL THOUGHTS

Successful implementation means attending to details as you follow your plan. Of course, nothing will go 100 percent smoothly, and every project encounters some bumps in the road. The more you plan ahead, though, the more likely you are to have anticipated and prepared for any obstacles before they become problems. Developing a project timeline and employing basic project management principles will help you sort through issues before they arise. Including a sound marketing plan will help you communicate effectively about the changes you are implementing.

Chapter Seven

Training Staff and Users

When introducing new technologies at the library, providing training for staffs and users to work with new devices and software can mean the difference between successful implementation and failure. When training is inadequate—or even nonexistent—we often see technology underutilized or even pushed to the side. Without training, staff members and users alike may be uncomfortable with the new hardware or software and may not understand how to utilize it. Librarians might complain, "This didn't fit our community's need" or, "No one was interested," but the real problem is more often a lack of appropriate education, not a lack of interest.

Training is an ongoing effort, not a onetime activity. Training for technology needs to be a planned, continual activity. Most technologies will evolve and change. Staff members and users will come and go, and new arrivals will need basic instruction. Even those who remain may need refresher training as well as updates on new versions or releases.

LOGISTICS OF TRAINING

One of the first decisions to make is choosing those who will lead the staff and user training. One person might be responsible for both types of training, but different people and even people from different departments could be involved. Also, decide whether the initial trainers will serve as the ongoing trainers or whether they will hand off the responsibility to someone else. One approach is to employ a train-the-trainer method to develop and deploy multiple trainers.

Training the staff and training the public are different tasks and need to occur at different times. Staff training should be the responsibility of an individual who is either a member of the implementation team or in close

communication with the team, who understands the implementation schedule, and who is able to complete training of all key staff members before the
hardware or software is available to the public. On the other hand, public
training needs to be coordinated with the public debut of the new technology.
Any training for the public should be planned and scheduled beforehand so it
can start immediately once the technology is introduced.

How Will Training Be Organized?

Those who will lead initial training have multiple options. In one approach,
similar to the role played by a project manager, the lead trainer assigns others
to conduct the training for staff. Alternatively, lead trainers may do all the
training themselves, often conducting multiple sessions and possibly at
multiple locations. There are several issues to consider in choosing the best
approach. If one staff member will train others, will this individual be responsible for organizing the overall training structure? If one individual is to
serve as primary trainer, how will that person acquire the information needed
to teach others? Will he or she need to take training elsewhere, to work with
the vendor, or to take time from other duties to develop the needed level of
expertise and preparation?

An alternative to having one staff member who trains others (at least
initially) would be to bring in the hardware or software vendor or another
third party to present the training. Beyond vendor training, there are multiple
third-party options for online and face-to-face training throughout the library
community. These include (but are not limited to) your state or regional
library association, the American Library Association, your state library
agency, local library cooperatives, and other professional groups; many of
these offer a spectrum of training for library staffs. In addition, local nonprofits such as meet-up groups, community maker groups, and schools or
local businesses may offer training in technology topics.

Another variation is the train-the-trainer approach. In this scenario, one
person (the vendor or other third-party or staff expert) first teaches those
who, in turn, will train others. The training focuses not just on the technology
but also on techniques for effectively presenting the material to others in a
training environment. Those who are trained to conduct training can then
adapt the material for their department or branch staff or for segments of the
public—youth, seniors, and so forth—who are expected to use the technology. In addition, trained staff members may create tutorials to instruct other
staff members and the public. The train-the-trainer model can be effective
because it disperses the training load among more staff members; however,
the library and the lead trainer should watch for any inconsistencies in the
quality or effectiveness of the training as skill levels may vary among trainers. These issues can be analyzed by evaluating training effectiveness and by

employing quality-control procedures such as evaluating training materials and spot-checking training sessions.

Deciding What Training Is Needed and Whom to Train

The important questions of what training is necessary and who needs to be trained can be difficult to answer. First, not everyone needs the same level of training. Of course, all staff members should have a basic orientation to the new technology, especially when the project is large and likely to attract a lot of attention. This orientation should ensure that everyone on staff understands the technology and its outcomes. Having staff members who are comfortable talking to library users and encouraging them to try out the technology is an important aspect of marketing.

Is it essential for all library staff members to know how to operate the technology? Should there be different layers of complexity in the training provided to staff members who have different responsibilities? It may be acceptable for some staff members to have only a rudimentary knowledge of the technology's potential, while others will need more advanced training. Consider, for example, who needs to know how to use Microsoft Windows 10? A 3-D printer? Adobe Creative Suite?

For an operating system upgrade like Windows 10, you may decide that everyone should receive in-depth training. On the other hand, if you're installing the library's first 3-D printer, you might determine that all staff members should receive introductory training so they can promote its use but that only staff members in the teen department will be required to take advanced training. With Adobe Creative Suite, you might feel that all public service people need in-depth training while others need a basic orientation so they can answer questions such as, "I need to create an app for my business. How do I do that?" In many cases the decision will be that all staff members should understand the software's basic uses and functionality but not everyone will need expert-level knowledge.

Even though it may not be necessary to train all staff in all departments on each technology, don't discourage anyone who may want to learn; allow them to attend training if they are interested. Self-motivation and the desire to learn should be encouraged in each employee.

DESIGNING EFFECTIVE TRAINING

Effective technology training requires analyzing an item of technology, considering how it will be used, and anticipating questions that are likely to be asked frequently about its use. When planning training in the use of a 3-D printer, for example, the goal might be to introduce the concept of 3-D design and to explain how to print 3-D objects. When planning a large-scale update in operating systems, the goal might be to explain new features of the software and any changes to the interface. When instructing the staff to use equipment in a small business center, the goal might be to help them understand what users can accomplish with the computers.

In determining the goal of the training, consider the audience. Who will be trained—the staff, community leaders, seniors, small business owners, teens? Which group is the target for each specific class, session, or workshop? If the focus is on a specific group, it will be easier to design effective training and, in many cases, to adapt the content and method of instruction to fit the audience. For example, a class on Microsoft Word for small business owners or job seekers might focus on résumés, one for senior adults might emphasize journaling, and one for teens could center on writing reports and essays.

When setting training goals, it's important to stay focused. Start by identifying the single, most important concept attendees should take away from this time period. Include only content that's relevant to the goal. While it can be tempting to jam in all you know about the subject, too much information—especially any tangential or off-message topics—can overwhelm attendees and reduce the training's effectiveness. As a trainer, your aim should be to keep the overall goal in mind while teaching what the student can absorb and retain, not to see how much can be covered within the time frame.

Training should focus only on the goal and should exclude extraneous material. This is not the time to toss in the proverbial kitchen sink. As an example, consider training on podcasting stations. The goal for a session could be to have attendees actually create a podcast. If so, focus on recording, editing, and publishing during the session. Other interesting topics, such as marketing podcasts or finding guest speakers to record, are not related to the goal; leave them out this time but consider them as subjects for additional training at a later date.

To decide how much material can be covered, determine the amount of time available for the class or workshop. The choice of an hour, ninety minutes, a half day, or a full day may involve multiple factors including the library's operating hours and the availability of space. Attendee availability is also a consideration; teens are not available until school ends, while professionals and hobbyists are more likely to attend weekend or evening programs and retirees may prefer daytime classes. In addition, reflect on any past training programs and allow their success or failure to guide you in selecting the most effective times within your library and community.

The longer the class, the more in-depth information that can be taught. A one-hour class can provide a general overview while a full-day class could feature full immersion in most aspects of the new technology and result in a deeper level of learning. Remember that regardless of the length of training, the main points should be repeated throughout and with different approaches.

Don't cram hours of content into a one-hour class. The pace of the session should support attendees' learning, not give them mental whiplash.

People have different learning styles. Some are visual learners while others prefer an auditory or kinesthetic approach. Successful training will include approaches for each style. Training should include visuals—the technology itself, slides, and possibly supplemental written materials. The information presented should include specific instructions; speaking clearly is especially important for auditory learners. All participants should have opportunities to touch and interact with the technology. Some students may prefer to watch a demonstration and then repeat the action themselves. After the instructor shows or demonstrates, allow participants to try it themselves.

With software, each trainee should be able to access the computer program on their own while in the class. With hardware, it's important to have the equipment fully operational and available during the training. Access to the equipment may be limited if there's only a single podcast station or 3-D printer. In these situations, participants may need to schedule a separate interactive training period for a later time. However, even if there's not an opportunity for each person to interact with the hardware, everyone should be able to spend at least a few minutes with it.

All methods of training should include an easy method for attendees to ask questions. Allowing users to get help quickly or to find additional information without difficulty can make the difference between successful and unsuccessful training. In a live class, there should be pauses for questions and answers frequently throughout the presentation. With on-demand learning, options for email, chat, or phone questions should be available to attendees. During staff training, you might include the trainer's direct contact information for attendees' follow-up questions. When training members of the public, it's usually better to provide general contact information for the library, including an email address and phone number where people can reach immediate assistance.

Effective training also includes a means of evaluation. How will you determine whether the training was effective? If the trainer was knowledgeable? To what extent the goal was met? The most common method for capturing this information is a survey distributed either on paper or by email. Along with the immediate feedback of an evaluation survey taken at the close of the training period, plan for additional feedback at a later time.

An additional follow-up survey done several months after the class can be especially helpful in determining the long-term effectiveness of the training. A second survey like this can be difficult to arrange with members of the public but can be valuable in evaluating staff training. A post-training survey can help determine whether those who were trained were actually able to help users with the technology in a satisfactory manner. After using the technology in the real world, staff members are better able to identify training gaps. They can suggest components to add to future training and can identify additional skills as the focus of later sessions. These evaluations should be reviewed by the lead trainers, by any pertinent committees within the library, and by the administrative staff.

Trainers should also have access to the evaluations of those in classes they lead so they can use that information to improve. Training is not a onetime activity. It should constantly evolve, engaging users and staff members to continually improve their skill sets.

TRAINING METHODS

There are multiple formats to consider when creating training for the staff or users. A blend of the following approaches, combined to meet the learning needs of each audience, will help reach people effectively.

In Person

In-person training is an effective way to bring new technology to life. Whether learning to create 3-D designs, to race robots, or to edit photos, attendees appreciate a hands-on experience that gives them an opportunity to gain a personal perspective on new hardware or software. However, there are challenges to this approach. Attendees must show up at a specific time and place to receive information. There must be an appropriate physical space available for the training. And for those new to the role of trainer, managing a classroom full of people can be difficult.

For in-person training, consider the logistics of the room or other space to be used. Ideally, the training session should take place where the technology is located. For example, when training on a new makerspace, podcast station, or small business resource center, the ideal site is where the equipment will be permanently situated. Logistically, though, this might not be feasible. Holding a class in an area normally available to the public can result in an inconvenience to library users who want to use the space and a less-than-ideal situation for training.

Realistically, the space available for training could be an off-site location, a different branch, or another space in the library. Prior to the day of training, make sure all the needed technology will work in the new area. Here's a checklist to use when setting up any training space, whether it's familiar or a new location.

• Is there adequate Wi-Fi? How do you connect to it? Can you connect all the devices as needed?

- Will you need electrical outlets? How many are available, and where are they located? Can they be reached easily and safely, or will you need to bring extension cords or surge protectors?
- Are you using software for the first time on a different computer? Check to make sure it loads and works correctly.
- Do you have the log-in information needed to connect to the software? Does it work properly on the computer you'll be using and in the physical location where the training will be held? Some software may be configured to allow access only by IP address or may be limited to certain devices, so make sure you have access to everything you need to use.

Plan for the physical setup of any room used for training. Each attendee who will have a device or who will use the technology hands-on will need a table. The most effective arrangement of tables will depend on the type of audience and the number of attendees. Classroom-style, u-shaped, square, or rectangle arrangements can all be effective. Classroom style is a formal arrangement where there is one instructor and attendees sit in rows; this style does not lend itself well to discussion. U-shaped, closed square, and rectangle configurations lend themselves to collaborative learning and discussion; however, these configurations work best for smaller groups.

Online Learning

One of the fastest growing trends in training is toward live online classes. These classes allow participants—presenters as well as attendees—to join the class from any computer connected to the Internet.

Online learning can be accomplished through a variety of software and cloud-based options. These include subscription systems like Adobe Connect and GoToWebinar; freemium software like Zoom, Skype, and JoinMe; and free alternatives like Google Hangouts. Each of these programs allows presenters to share their computer screens and applications. Class members are able to ask questions and interact with the presenter.

Online learning can be as effective as in-person learning if the instructor utilizes appropriate software and follows recognized best practices for presentations. Recommended tips for successful online training include the following:

- Test all components. Presenters should do both visual and sound checks within the online meeting software in advance of the class. This is to ensure microphone levels are appropriate, visuals load and display correctly, and any live demonstrations will work as intended.
- Engage the audience. To keep them involved and focused on the training, attendees should be given tasks to perform regularly throughout the class;

tasks can vary from completing quizzes to raising their hands virtually and to answering questions.
- Involve multiple voices. A copresenter can be especially effective in increasing the effectiveness of training. A second person who moderates questions, helps with technical issues, and provides a change of voice can produce a higher level of attendee engagement.
- Remember the visual. In a traditional classroom, the focus is generally on the instructor. In a virtual classroom, one without a trainer present, the audience needs a focal point so the visual elements must be provided on the screen. To hold participants' interest, presenters should change slides often and blend slides with screenshots and live demonstrations where possible.
- Describe the screen. When providing a live demonstration or discussing screenshots, the presenter should make sure to explain each step of the process.

Classes conducted online can often be recorded and the recordings used for on-demand learning at a later time.

On-Demand Learning

On-demand learning provides staff members and users with training on their schedule. It is available with the click of a mouse and can be an effective option for training both staffs and users. When time and budgets are limited, on-demand training can be the best way to reach the most people. Many on-demand training pieces may be used for both staffs and users, although the content may need to be adapted somewhat.

A library of on-demand resources for users and staffs can be arranged in a variety of ways. These resources are often seen on different websites as an "FAQ" section, as instructional help screens, or as video tutorials. Any of these three can be effective in meeting immediate user demand. The best scenario blends all three methods into a robust on-demand platform.

Content for online learning should be in a form that is practical, findable, and easy to use. Any on-demand training should focus only on a specific task or the present issue. For example, a series of short tutorials that focus on individual components is more effective than a longer presentation that describes all the features of a device or software program. Consider tutorials that the City Library might provide for those using its new podcasting stations. Short segments on practical topics might include how to record, how to perform a sound check, or how to edit sound, while another segment might outline best practices for a podcast.

Few people are willing to watch a long video on a help topic or to read a long list of instructions. Most want to get straight to the information they need, and to do so at the time they need it. Brief on-demand explanations of high-interest topics make learning easier. This style of learning is called "chunking" because the material to be learned is grouped into chunks—smaller, digestible bites that the learner can easily process. With chunking, learners can work through an entire series of topics for in-depth training on a specific resource or can pick and choose the aspects they need to achieve their goals.

FAQs and Written Tutorials

When writing tutorials for an FAQ page or creating a knowledge base for the staff and users, ensure the text is written so that those who are browsing for information can find what they need quickly. Include these elements:

- To maximize the usability of on-demand content, include a search option as well as browsable content organization for ease in locating the desired information.
- Use headings as well as numbers or bullet points.
- Keep descriptions brief; remove unnecessary words. Paragraphs should be short. Only include information the user needs.
- Use annotated screenshots whenever possible. A screenshot is a "capture" or picture of a browser window or mobile screen. Screenshots should include only relevant information; delete any extraneous information such as browser bookmarks, plugins, or images of the desktop. Arrows and pointers can be added to highlight buttons and other key features.
- Make written tutorials easily available as web content by embedding them on the library's website. Avoid placing these tutorials in PDF or other formats that may become barriers to findability and accessibility.

Video Tutorials

Video tutorials are another growing trend in training, one that's replacing written FAQ documents; it's a trend that's likely to continue. A video tutorial demonstrates how to move from one step to the next. A series of short videos is a user-friendly way to show the learner the entire process.

Videos may be created in-house, but there exists a multitude of options created by vendors and others who have used the devices or software. Before starting to develop materials just for your library, research those training materials that are already available. Are there vendor resources that will meet your needs? Adobe, for example, has a robust video library available on their website. Consider curating a list of vendor resources and adding links to them on your website or help area. Videos on YouTube may be another useful option.

If you decide to design your own materials, here are keys to developing good video tutorials.

- Each video in the series should focus on a specific task and should be less than five minutes in length. Shorter is even better.
- Explain each step as you perform it. Stating the details of what you're doing creates a more useful video. For instance, saying, "Click on the blue button labeled Print that's located on the bottom of the screen" is more useful than just saying, "Now print." This level of detail is especially helpful for users with visual impairments or others trying to mirror your tutorial.
- Script the video before recording. Know each step in the process, what screens will appear, and which will display as the result of a specific search. Plan what you will say with each step as it is shown. Training videos should be straight to the point; there is no room for "dead air" or unexplained pauses as you read the screen and decide what to do. Avoid accidentally clicking on the wrong item; this can confuse and frustrate the learner. Scripting the video first will also help identify information that may be needed, such as example log-ins or library card numbers and may alert you to software updates that are needed for everything to work correctly.
- When recording instructions, speak slowly and clearly.

If you rely on on-demand learning, make sure your training content remains up to date. Many technical products, especially cloud-based software, constantly evolve. Ensure the training materials reflect the current version of the software. Software updates can cause buttons to move, interfaces to change, and functionality to be altered. Out-of-date training videos will frustrate your users and staff members.

Record analytical data on how many times tutorials are accessed. One way to do this is with Google Analytics Tag Manager, a system for tagging specific links within your site for in-depth analytics. Video-hosting platforms also provide their own analytics. This data reveals whether a tutorial is watched, where and when it's viewed, and whether the viewer watched the entire video or stopped early—and at what point. Even more important, analytics indicate what has not been watched. Analytics will show what training options are used and will provide hard data to supplement any anecdotal information. This will show where skill gaps exist among your staff and users and will provide a better picture of how the training is being used as well as what additional training is needed.

There are many software options for creating video tutorials. To create quick, short videos, consider free options for screen recording such as Tech-Smith's Jing and the open-source Cam Studio. These free versions do not allow for editing; if even one word must be changed, the video must be rerecorded. If you plan to create videos for both users and the staff, editable software may save time. In these cases, consider paid versions such as PowerPoint's native recording feature, Camtasia, or the free operating system options: Apple's iMovie and Windows Movie Maker. When evaluating software for purchase, consider the ease of use when editing a video as well as the purchase price. To record an app on a mobile device, there are multiple apps for Android and Apple with the native ability to record your screen.

Make videos designed for training users and staffs as accessible as possible. An effective practice is to dedicate a page on your library's website as a hub for all on-demand technology training. However, hosting videos on the library's site may create a heavy load on your server, so explore alternatives. For example, video-hosting services such as YouTube, Vimeo, and LibGuides and hosting platforms like Niche Academy can be more efficient and less problematic in the long run. Links to these platforms can be embedded in the library's own web page for quick access.

CREATING EFFECTIVE STAFF TRAINING
WITH ACCOUNTABILITY

Training the staff on new technology is an absolute must if you want the technology to succeed. No amount of marketing can compensate for staff members who are unable to assist users with equipment or software. With training, there needs to be accountability for the staff, to ensure not only that they attended, viewed, or read training materials but also that they understood the training and developed the skills needed to use and assist users with the new technology.

Creating face-to-face or in-person instruction for staffs can be logistically challenging for most libraries; it's often impossible for all employees to attend training at the same time because doing so would mean leaving public areas unattended. Therefore, for any training needed by all staff members, libraries need to design multiple opportunities. Depending on the library's size, the trainer may need to travel to multiple locations or to offer sessions at several times to ensure everyone is trained. As discussed earlier, it may not be necessary for all staff members to attend all training. For example, a librarian at the Beach Library may need orientation training on only robotics for the makerspace at City Library. Therefore, a blended solution that combines online orientation with completing a basic task might be the most effective way to ensure each person receives the right amount of training. This could work well, for example, when providing introductory-level training in software like Adobe. More in-depth, on-demand training or live classes may be required for those who will work directly with the software and will assist users.

Establishing training goals and determining a way to evaluate progress toward those goals are necessary for effective training and overall staff accountability. Did the staff watch the required training? Did they pay attention? Most importantly, did they learn the key points about the technology? Will they be able to assist users? Can they use the technology competently? Are they able to troubleshoot problems with the technology? On-demand training should include a strong evaluation component to determine its effectiveness. We will explore several different methodologies that can be used to create models for accountable training.

Learning Management Systems

A learning management system (LMS) is a formal system that can be used to create a continuing education program for all staff members. An LMS allows the head trainer to develop courses that blend live instruction, video, and text-based learning. Topics can be set up as courses and may include quizzes, bulletin board discussions, and graded assignments. The LMS provides reports to managers and makes it apparent who is achieving training goals and who is not. Younger employees will likely have used an LMS in college and may already be comfortable in this type of learning environment. For older employees, a library LMS may present their first experience with the software.

An LMS is not ideal for onetime training. It works best as an ongoing tool that augments existing training and formalizes on-demand instruction. Multiple vendors, including Captivate, Canvas, Blackboard, and Bridge for Teams, provide learning management systems. Moodle is an open-source alternative. When evaluating LMS software, balance cost with ease of use. Also, consider the overall management process and features to be used by course instructors and the staff. All LMS systems should provide a trial period for evaluating the software before purchase.

Interactive Stand-Alone Training

Techsmith's Camtasia and Articulate Storyline are two different software platforms that allow the user to create single-session interactive training units. These bring interactivity to on-demand presentations with the capability of including quizzes, allowing the learner to select objects on the screen and providing other learning checks. The trainee reads the slides or watches interactive videos and is then prompted to complete a task that ensures they've learned the content designated as a takeaway. For example, when a new printer is added to the reference department, training may be designed to teach staff members to load it with ink. An interactive training unit may include a quiz or display an image that learners click to show they understand where the ink is placed in the printer. Sessions like these can be created as stand-alone training or added to an LMS as part of a more comprehensive plan.

Developing a Training Intranet or Web Presence

A library of on-demand training should be placed in an accessible, user-friendly place for staff convenience. The effort put into creating training units is wasted if they are scattered throughout shared drives or dispersed in emails and then lost by the recipients. Designate an area for hosting content on your staff intranet or on a simple website. This website could host locally produced content, provide access to vendor information, and include documentation for additional support. To keep the library's technology assessment current, this information should also be added to the technology inventory that was originally developed.

While a website or staff intranet may not include the formal interaction capability of an LMS, it can still provide analytics. If the materials on the website are from a training tutorial, require trainees to log in or have them submit a note of completion once the training is finished. Within a website, the staff can be required to comment on the training, to log in before accessing materials, or to complete a freestanding quiz that supplements an on-demand video.

Additional Options

Adding Feedback to Other Forms of Training

A less formal but still effective method of evaluating the effectiveness of training and the new skill levels of attendees is to use the same style of on-demand materials discussed above but to add a task, quiz, checklist, or other feedback method to ensure the training goal was met. Although these options may empower staff members to determine for themselves whether the training was effective, the analytics available to management would include fewer details. In a hypothetical situation, for example, Maggie from the reference department would watch on-demand training about the new podcast station. She must watch a series of videos that explain how to record, edit, upload, and publish a podcast. Ideally, after Maggie completes this training, she would be required to create and upload a podcast. If doing so would require too much time, you may decide a quiz or checklist of skills would be a sufficient means of accountability.

Training via Email

Not all training must be formal. When implementing small-scale changes to technology such as software updates, it may be possible to convey necessary information via email. Email can also be an effective way to deliver small bites of ongoing training to help the staff understand changes in functionality. This approach, which allows staff members to learn on their own schedule, may therefore be more efficient.

An email message should be designed following the same principles outlined in the "FAQs and Written Tutorials" section in "On-Demand Learning" earlier in this chapter. Focus on brevity, easy reading, and visual aids. Once sent, the content of the message should be archived in an accessible location so it can be found after the recipient has deleted the original email.

A training bite sent via email should contain the product name followed by a short description of the improvement, functionality, or training feature to be explained. You may also decide to brand these emails so the subject line is fairly standard, for example, Quick Tips: A Look at the New Ozobot, or Training Bytes: Cleaning the 3-D Printer. A video or photo to highlight the feature's functionality would be helpful as would directions for finding more information or support, either internally or from the vendor.

Gamification in Training

Gamification, or adding games or gamelike activities, is yet another option to bring accountability to staff training. For example, online badging, which is a method of providing digital badges for accomplishments, can add incentives for continual learning. In the real world, these online badges can translate into prizes, into archived benchmarks considered in annual performance evaluations, and into bragging rights for staff.

Gamification can help create "buzz" around new training and technology and can help the staff see how others utilize training options. It's only successful, though, when you create a culture around it and encourage the gaming. If games are only an overlay on the LMS and there's little promotion or engagement, buy-in by staff will be low.

DESIGNING USER TRAINING THAT WORKS

Effective training for users may take different forms depending on the different technologies deployed within your library and on the variety of software that users can borrow or access remotely. Those who will use 3-D printers, podcasting stations, or job resource computers will likely need in-person training as will users who are baby boomers or older, those with low comfort levels with technology, and anyone who will use complex technical devices.

On the other hand, web-based training may work well for technologies that users can access remotely, although those same technologies may also require face-to-face training. On-demand sessions can work well for either home-based or in-library users working with technologies where the interface makes it easy to get started but where help is often needed to use advanced features.

BECOMING COMFORTABLE AS A TRAINER

Not everyone is naturally comfortable in the role of trainer. Before taking on training responsibilities, many library staff members will need to develop the skills for voice recording or for presenting in a web-based or live classroom environment. These formats are inherently different from assisting users individually and in person at a service desk.

Successful trainers must plan the training in advance, script presentations describing hardware or software, and prepare to speak to a group. For those who need to develop the ability to speak comfortably in public, look to outside groups like Toastmasters International for training and encouragement to master this skill, one that will help them with both technology training and overall success as a librarian.

FINAL THOUGHTS

Employing the forms of training described in this chapter can ensure the successful implementation of new technologies at your library. Most likely a blended solution that brings together multiple techniques will prove to be the most effective approach in training staffs and users.

To use new technology properly, users and staff members alike need opportunities for hands-on experience. With on-demand training, it is vital to provide an environment where staff members and users also have ready access to the technology. Simply watching videos or reading about the new robotics program or 3-D printer will not become meaningful until people can see and use the technology in real life.

No training is truly effective without follow-up. For the implementation of technology to remain successful beyond the initial buzz, develop an ongoing strategy to train both staffs and users.

Chapter Eight

Maintaining Technology

In the previous chapter, we focused on the importance of developing a training strategy for both the library's users and its staff. We mentioned that technology continues to evolve with new features, uses, and versions. Your technology plan will guide you through the crucial early stages of implementing new technologies, but your plan should also address maintaining and supporting that technology over time.

In this chapter, we will explore the need to create and execute a maintenance plan for each item of technology within your library. Developing a plan for maintenance is especially important if you do not have dedicated IT staff.

This chapter includes a look at updating software and hardware and at managing staff resources to minimize downtime and service interruptions. We will explore what is involved in maintaining technology and the staffing requirements needed to implement a workable maintenance plan that is integrated into the library's day-to-day operations.

UPDATING TECHNOLOGY

A major maintenance concern is managing software and hardware updates. Updates may be released daily, weekly, or monthly while others are issued less frequently or even rarely. Regardless of the release schedule, updates are vital for any technology to work correctly. Not only are they essential to fix security vulnerabilities and bugs, but also they can add new features to the software or hardware.

Every type of hardware and software must be monitored so that new updates can be installed in a timely manner. Software vendors and hardware providers rank the types of updates; these rankings will help you determine when the update should be installed. For example, a "critical update," usually one that contains security fixes, needs to be installed promptly. On the other hand, minor updates to fix less critical software bugs, such as display issues, may not be as urgent.

Updates can be installed in three main ways. Your library may select one method but more likely will prefer a blended solution that uses aspects of each option. These options are as follows:

- Centralized management software that pushes updates to individual computers
- Manual updates that are installed directly on the actual device through software loaded on a thumb drive or SD card or via a connected computer
- Automatic updates that are installed when the software detects a new version. This can be arranged via a default setting or as an optional setting within the software or device. With cloud-based solutions, automatic updates are often the default.

Let's explore these three scenarios and the circumstances under which each method works best.

Centralized Management Software

One of the benefits of centralized management software is that it allows one person or department to push out updates from one location and to easily identify computers that may be missing updates or security patches. Centralized management systems were explained in chapter 3. To review, these systems are not only for managing software updates; they also include other benefits such as server monitoring, new software installation, security, and storage updates. For libraries with a considerable number of computer workstations or computers housed in multiple locations and departments, a centralized system can be a vital tool for efficient management from a single location.

When considering the addition of a centralized management system, it is important to first step back and analyze your staff's expertise. These systems are very complex to set up. A knowledgeable IT person is needed to run a centralized system properly. If your library lacks this level of staff expertise, outsourcing this management might be an alternative. Outsourcing may be a viable option when a library has a significant amount of technology or if its staff lacks the necessary time or expertise to carry out maintenance tasks. For libraries considering contracting for maintenance by outside vendors, we will explore how to evaluate IT companies later in this chapter.

Manual Updates

Firmware is the software that runs a device. Routers, servers, printers, 3-D printers, and makerspace resources are all examples of hardware that may require updates to their operating systems; many of these will require manual installation of updates. Firmware updates often fix bugs to the operating system, repair security vulnerabilities, and may even improve the user interface or general functionality of the hardware. With routers and other infrastructure hardware, it is especially imperative that staff members are proactive in monitoring updates.

The frequency of firmware update releases and the best method for installing those updates will vary depending on the device. Some can be managed centrally while other hardware—peripherals and makerspace resources, for example—may require manual updates.

Finding information on available firmware updates is not always easy. How do you find out about these updates? Equipment vendors will post notices on their website and send messages through a mailing list; thus, the staff needs to monitor both venues. The staff members who are responsible for updates will need to sign up for mailing lists and check periodically for updates on the vendor's website.

Manual updates require that a person is physically next to the hardware and available to intervene manually to initiate the updates. Depending on the number of computers to be updated, this method can be quite time consuming. It is not a feasible solution if a library has more than just a few computers. Because updates need to be installed regularly and in a timely manner, this method is impractical in environments with large numbers of computers and with only one individual available to conduct the installations. Under such circumstances the job would never be completed, the systems would be vulnerable to security issues, and the library would have multiple versions of software running on different machines—an arrangement that can cause confusion for both users and the staff.

For libraries without a formal IT department or a centralized management system, one solution—while not ideal—is to create a cross-department or cross-location team that is responsible for managing computers. Team members can assist one another with notifications and with addressing issues while sharing the responsibility for updating individual computers. A team approach also helps to provide staff coverage for vacations and other situations where staffing may be limited. In addition, this approach can help in planning for succession by providing training and hands-on experience, allowing several in-house individuals to develop greater technical expertise.

Leaving all manual updates to one individual is generally not a good idea, unless the task is that person's only responsibility. There is a limit to the number of manual updates that any one person can manage effectively. Relying only on this approach is not a scalable solution; as the library adds more computers or other forms of technology, it will not be possible to keep up with the increased workload if all updates must be manually installed. Your staff will not be able to maintain the library's technology properly if there is too much that must be done manually. Symptoms of the need for a more scalable solution include reaching points where multiple versions of software are in use, a higher proportion of technical issues are occurring, or staff members are beginning to stress over the challenge of keeping abreast of updates. When any of these occur, consider centralized management software. Even if a central system had been considered in the past but was thought to be too expensive or complex, it may be time to reevaluate that decision.

In addition to manual updates for software, the firmware for hardware also needs to be updated. While some firmware may be updated through the centralized management system, it's likely that, at least part of the time, firmware updates will need to be installed directly on a local computer or other device.

As you add technology to the library, be sure to understand how firmware updates will be received and how they are to be installed. Often firmware updates are not pushed out by the manufacturer as seamlessly as software updates. In fact, considering the ways in which firmware and software are to be updated should be an evaluation point in any technology purchase decision.

Auto-Updates with Cloud-Based Software

Cloud-based systems automatically install updates, including security patches, so users will always have access to the newest version of the software. Whenever a newer version of the software is available, the software is updated as it opens. In addition, cloud software is often able to manage files, including backups, with little downtime. If your library staff lacks the expertise to manage software locally, consider cloud-based software among the maintenance options you evaluate. The overall advantage of cloud-based office tools, photo editors, and other specialized software is the lack of need for local maintenance. If you feel cloud-based solutions will work well for your library, you may also want to seek cloud-based alternatives to popular software. For example, cloud-based options for Microsoft Office include Microsoft 365, Google Drive, and Zoho.

While some cloud-based software options auto-update, it may be possible to schedule others to run at designated times. Still others may require a manual update. For most products, including web browsers and operating systems, updates may be pushed to your computer automatically but can then be installed on your preferred schedule. If updates are scheduled in advance, they can be run during off hours or at other times when a computer is not being used by the staff or the public. Scheduling updates is usually an option found in the preferences or settings for the software. Note that, if you decide not to allow automatic installation of updates, the responsibility for downloading and installing the updates shifts to the staff.

Updates help protect your library from security threats. They should be applied in a timely fashion; this is especially true for any that contain patches for security issues. Regardless of how you choose to deal with updates, they should not be ignored.

KEEPING TECHNOLOGY SECURE

Protecting against Malicious Attacks

Updates are just one important line of defense in protecting your library from security threats. Cybersecurity is one of the biggest challenges facing libraries today and will continue to be a concern for the foreseeable future. The all-too-real threats from malware, ransomware, and other malicious activity, which were defined and explained in chapter 2, exploit known issues in software or operating systems. These threats can jeopardize the library's network, data (both the library's own data and that of users) and day-to-day operations. The damage by security breaches can be expensive and can result in lost data and a loss of public trust. Take these threats seriously.

Keeping all the library's technology safe can be a daunting task. The main sources of vulnerability to data breaches can be mitigated with good policies, software updates, and staff education. Five primary areas for system vulnerability include the following:

- Phishing attacks. Email messages may lure the staff to reveal information such as the log-in details that provide access to their own accounts.
- Malicious injections. A harmful file is sent via download or a link inside an email. These may be sent randomly or directed specifically to targeted staff members.
- Network access by unauthorized devices. Administrators must decide which devices will be allowed to connect to the library's network and which will not. For example, only "official" library computers and other devices should be allowed to connect to the critical staff network. Personal devices of staff members should be limited to the public Wi-Fi and not be allowed on the staff network. This was discussed in more detail in chapter 3 as part of creating a sound network policy.
- Failure to update software and firmware. Vulnerabilities are discovered regularly in software and firmware. As these are identified, manufacturers

develop patches to correct the problems. If you fail to install these updates, your system is open to known security issues.

- Ineffective management of staff accounts, especially those of former staff members. Have a plan of action ready when staff members leave the library's employment. Remove their accounts from the management of software and firmware, and provide vendors with new contact information for accounts as needed. Forward the former employee's email account to a supervisor for a set number of days; then delete the email account. If the employee had access to an account shared with one or more other employees, change the password or pin. Leaving old accounts in place gives hackers an easy way to access your software, firmware, and network.

The best approach for ensuring a secure system is to adopt sound maintenance policies and to ensure those policies are implemented consistently. For example, when setting up the network on the router, you likely created multiple networks, each with different levels of access and security. Perhaps these levels were designated as "Admin," "Staff," and "Public Wi-Fi." You then determined which devices should be allowed to connect to each network. As time goes by, you need to make sure the original choices are still the right choices and that each item is configured correctly. For example, was a printer or computer connected to the public Wi-Fi when it should have been assigned to a more secure staff network on the router? Review the devices that are running on each network, and check that each device is assigned appropriately. This evaluation is especially important when adding new equipment.

Review and adjust settings to your router as needed. This doesn't mean you should change the settings just for the sake of change, but it is important to review daily activities within your library. Adjust network settings so that all security issues are monitored and your network is secure. Changes to the settings of a computer or its peripherals are made frequently and easily, but the decision to make a change must be an intentional one, not one done incorrectly or in error.

To further ensure your network is safe, the person responsible for the library's technology needs to look beyond official updates for vulnerabilities that do not have an official fix. There are several websites and user forums that the staff can join to find out about vulnerabilities and the steps that can be taken to mitigate a security flaw until an official patch is available from the vendor. Here are some examples of websites to follow:

- User forums for the specific device. For example, there may be a user group for hardware or software the library uses. These user groups, while not offering an official solution, will often have short-term fixes for new problems as they arise.

- The Open Web Application Security Project (Owasp.org). This nonprofit organization is dedicated to providing impartial information on security issues through a group of volunteers.
- National Vulnerability Database (Nvd.nist.gov). This repository of software vulnerabilities is operated by the US government. The site provides information on technology issues and the status of efforts to resolve them.
- ThreatPost (threatpost.com). With a user-friendly interface, this site publishes reports on vulnerabilities and security issues for popular software.

Physical Security

Protecting items from theft should also be an ongoing and evolving process. There are several ways to protect against users walking out with technology. The level of security will vary depending on what you are protecting and on your community. The most basic protection is to add a security tag to every possible device. This will alert the staff if one is removed from the building.

Large items such as computer monitors, printers, and CPUs can be physically locked down to prevent them from being moved; lockdown plates, anchors, and cable locks are effective for this purpose. Peripherals—such as mice and keyboards—for these devices may be locked with small security locks. Some libraries may find these are necessary steps while others will feel secure without these measures.

More portable devices—such as gaming controllers, laptops, Ozobots, and Spheros—may require a more hands-on approach. Here are three options:

- Place small items like LittleBits, Legos, and Ozobots in an area visible to the staff. This requires a level of trust with users but provides the most access to the technologies.
- Barcode the devices, and require that users check them out for in-house use. This requires staff time for managing checkouts but overall gives users availability and flexibility of use for devices. Checkout can also help with accountability for those who may damage technology (Dockery 2017).
- Some libraries choose to allow use of technologies only during programs. This is the most restrictive option as it limits the usage.

To help prevent theft, make sure all technology is documented and covered under the library's insurance policy.

MOVING TO NEW VERSIONS OF SOFTWARE

Software manufacturers frequently update their products. Some updates (or new versions) contain relatively few changes while others may be much more extensive. A new version is typically labeled as a new software version while updates are identified with decimal numbers. For example, Adobe Acrobat Version 12.0 is a new version, while 12.1.2 is an update to the more extensive Version 12.0. Vendors and software companies usually promote major upgrades to new versions widely and well in advance, as when Microsoft announced its Windows 10 operating system. Large-scale upgrades of this type bring a wide array of changes for users.

In libraries, upgrading computers to a new operating system requires advanced planning. It's important that the installation is completed in a timely manner, and it may be necessary to schedule a specific time for system-wide turnovers. Implementing a significant upgrade often means that computers and software will be unavailable while machines are updating. You may decide to restrict computers from use or to conduct updates when the library is closed.

New versions of software often require some staff orientation or training too. In chapter 7, we discussed the importance of designating the person or persons responsible for leading training for the staff and users. The person who takes the lead for software training will need to evaluate the new version first to decide what level of training is appropriate. For instance, a version update in Adobe may contain only minor modifications; in this case, a quick email to alert staff (and possibly users) to new features or interface changes may be adequate. On the other hand, a complete overhaul of core software—such as the ILS or the Windows operating system—may warrant a series of training sessions.

As each new version of software is announced—and especially with more extensive updates—review any related support documents that have been previously posted online for the library staff and users. Also, review the content of related training to ensure that information is still accurate.

Before updating any software, review its technical requirements and evaluate them. Older hardware may not be able to adapt to the requirements of new software, and performance problems can result. You will need to evaluate whether new versions of software signal the end of life for other technology within your library or whether they are likely to cause an issue with other software or hardware. For example, a new operating system may cause compatibility issues with an older printer. Does the computer on which the new software will be installed have enough RAM (processing power) necessary to run this software version? Are other underlying programs, such as Flash or Java, required for the software to run properly? If so, do these programs need to be updated as well?

Sometimes a major update can require more resources than are available on existing hardware. In some cases, a new version of software may even signal the end of the manufacturer's support for earlier versions of hardware or software. Before you start a migration, ensure the device can handle the new version.

Some system updates can create compatibility issues with existing software. Before launching a system-wide update, it is best to test the update on one computer with your library's current software installed to evaluate whether there are any compatibility issues. Possible root causes of incompatibility include the following:

- Obsolete software. One issue that can arise is when an operating system update breaks the older software, which is no longer being updated or maintained by its developer and which cannot run with a modern operating system or browser. If this happens, you need to decide if it's critical to keep the older software or if it can be replaced by more modern software. If you need to keep the software, is there a work-around that will allow its continued use? Ignoring updates to keep a software running is not a long-term solution.
- Updates needed. Just before or after the release of a major software update, such as that for operating systems and browsers for computers and tablets, you will frequently see a large number of updates to applications made by other companies. These application updates are often released to resolve bugs or conflicts that arise with the new operating software.
- Bugs in the new software. While updates need to be installed in a timely manner, there's no need to be the first to launch a large update. It's best to wait at least a few days after the release before beginning an update. This allows time for others to identify any initial bugs and for the manufacturer to release a patch to correct them. When implementing a large update, try it out on one computer first; if all goes well and the computer is operating smoothly with the new software, then deploy the update throughout the library.

PHYSICAL MAINTENANCE

Software can almost always be maintained through updates. Hardware, on the other hand, often requires regular physical maintenance to prevent problems from arising. The range of physical maintenance tasks includes lubricating 3-D printers or cleaning devices such as printers, Ozobots, and mice. Here are a few examples: a computer's hardware, especially the areas around ports, should be cleaned several times a year with compressed air to clear out dust; the monitor should be wiped at least weekly with a microfiber cloth;

and the keyboard and mouse should be cleaned weekly to remove germs and grime.

Even though the physical maintenance of technology devices can be time consuming and labor intensive, this important task should be scheduled and completed regularly by the staff or a third-party vendor. Most hardware manufacturers provide a suggested schedule for ongoing maintenance of their products. If a specific item of hardware arrives without these instructions, look for the information on the manufacturer's website or the website of any community forum for the product.

Technology products in libraries are used more frequently and receive harder use than items limited to individual use. Because of the wear and tear library equipment receives, it's important to extend its lifespan as long as possible through proper maintenance. Without maintenance, there will be more downtime due to technical problems; these may include such issues as a printer that prints random lines, a 3-D printer that jams, or malfunctions caused by dirt in robotics, mice, or other hardware.

With larger and more complex technology like large printers/scanners, it may be economically beneficial, in terms of both expertise and time, to contract for maintenance with a company whose technicians are authorized by the equipment brand.

CREATING A MAINTENANCE CHECKLIST

Each maintenance activity needs to be assigned to the staff so there is accountability. For example, one note in the technology plan might be a simple statement such as, "Windows updates will be managed through active directory, by the IT department." Another note might be even more specific, as in, "The Afinia h800 3-D printer will be maintained by the full-time children's department librarian II (currently Samantha Smith)."

It's not sufficient, though, to simply assign the task to an individual. A better method is to create a formal maintenance checklist. A checklist is one of the easiest ways to ensure that regular maintenance and updates are performed. The checklist should specify what needs to be done, by whom it should be done, and how often it should be done. A good checklist makes it easy to see whether actions were completed.

As an example, let's look at the adult services area at Beach Library. This area has twelve public computers; all have the Windows 10 operating system, Microsoft Office, and both the Firefox and Edge browsers. To ensure the computers' operation and configuration files are protected and that any data added to the computers is wiped clean between users, all twelve are running Deep Freeze (http://www.faronics.com/products/deep-freeze). A thirteenth computer, reserved for the staff to manage literacy services, has the same configuration but does not have Deep Freeze. One additional computer, used by the public for genealogy research, has access to several specialized databases. The adult services area also has a large printer/scanner and a small makerspace. The makerspace includes two Macintosh computers with Deep Freeze installed; one computer is connected to a 3-D printer and the other has Adobe Suite installed. The makerspace also has twelve Ozobots on a work table with Android tablets.

Below is an example of scheduled maintenance tasks for the technology used by the public in Beach Library's adult services area. As you will see, even without considering staff software and hardware, there is a lot of maintenance work to be done.

Weekly:

- Install updates from Microsoft, including any updates for the operating system, Microsoft Office, and the Edge browser.
- Update antivirus software.
- Install updates from Firefox when available.
- Clean monitor with microfiber cloth.
- Clean and disinfect mice and keyboards with antibacterial wipes.
- Update Deep Freeze as needed.
- Run data backup of literacy computer.
- Check and install firmware updates for printer and 3-D printer.
- Check and install firmware updates for Ozobots.
- Check and install updates for Makerspace tablets.
- Install updates on two Macintosh computers.
- Install updates to Adobe Suite in makerspace.
- Check ink levels on printer.
- Inventory and order printer supplies, including paper and ink, as necessary.
- Inventory and order 3-D printer supplies, including filament, as necessary.

Monthly:

- Run full antivirus scan of literacy and genealogy computers.
- Clean 3-D printer nozzle and oil components.
- Clean and disinfect Ozobots.

Quarterly:

- On literacy computer, run a disc defragmentation and clean the registry.
- Deep clean the 3-D printer.
- Clean power supplies and check backup batteries.

A spreadsheet is the easiest way to keep track of each task, which can then be marked off as it's completed. An alternative to a spreadsheet would be a task management system like Trello or Zoho Projects.

Most importantly, each task should be assigned to a specific individual; this helps ensure accountability. Otherwise, experience has proven that updates will not be installed and devices will not be cleaned.

ASSIGNING RESPONSIBILITY

At the end of the day, it is important that every item of technology is assigned to a department. Further, someone within that department must be assigned to monitor and troubleshoot the technology and to train others in its use. Depending on the staff available, the responsible person may be someone from a team dedicated to IT or may be individuals within specific departments.

Maintenance responsibilities should be formally assigned, not put in the category of "when you have the time." If maintenance is not treated as a critical function, it will most likely not be performed. With staff input, determine how much time needs to be allocated. For example, "X hours a week should be reserved to do routine maintenance on the makerspace hardware."

In assigning maintenance and troubleshooting responsibilities to individuals, keep in mind each person's current job responsibilities and whether they need to acquire new skills if they are to be effective. When assigning duties, be mindful of the time necessary to complete the new task too. Evaluate whether other job responsibilities should be removed and reassigned to different staff members.

The benefit of maintenance will be directly proportional to the effort put in by the staff. With regular maintenance and updates, there will be fewer maintenance issues, performance problems, or unexpected downtime.

Staff Training for Maintenance

In addition to allocating staff time to maintenance tasks, make sure all designated staff members receive any training necessary to manage hardware and software appropriately. When considering technology purchases, be sure to find out what training is offered by the vendor. At a minimum, most vendors provide some opportunity to learn more about their products; these opportunities may be in the form of on-demand learning, webinars, live training, or conferences. Other vendors will offer more formal learning programs and even certifications.

While staff members may not need official certification, it's crucial that they have the knowledge necessary to manage the technology. If appropriate training isn't available from the vendor, look to your local IT community, library training sources, and third-party companies. Whether the people assigned to maintain equipment are IT professionals or other library staff, becoming knowledgeable about maintenance functions and staying abreast of developments should be a specific part of their job requirements.

Outsourcing Maintenance

Your library may decide it is more effective to outsource all or part of its technology maintenance. Having a third party manage specific software or hardware items or all the library's technology can make sense if you lack the internal staff resources to keep abreast of this important work. There are different ways to locate qualified companies. For large printers and other complex hardware items, there may often be a manufacturer-approved list of maintenance vendors. Alternatively, you may be able to locate a local technology maintenance company or a library-specific vendor.

If you decide to engage a third-party contractor to provide support and maintenance for any of the library's equipment, there must also be a specific staff liaison who communicates with that contractor. Instructions for contacting support for the contractor should be readily available to frontline staff. Allowing the staff to start support tickets (especially on nights and weekends) will help expedite support and ensure that software and hardware perform as expected in the long run.

When arranging for outside maintenance, protect the library with a written agreement describing the services to be performed and the performance standard expected of the vendor. No matter who the third party vendor is, it's important to have a formal agreement that lays out expectations for both parties. A contract or service-level agreement (SLA), even a simple one-page document, can clarify assumptions and prevent misunderstandings.

Here are some points to consider before agreeing to an SLA or contract:

- Staff. How many people does the vendor have on staff? What are their credentials? Understand the size of the company and how they will be able to respond to your needs. Is this a one-person shop, or does the company have a team for support?
- Location. Is the company local? If you need physical maintenance and support, proximity is important. If remote support is sufficient, this factor should weigh less prominently.
- Method. Does the contractor provide on-site support or only remote assistance? If on-site support is available, are additional costs involved?
- Scope. What services are included? Will the contractor provide general, routine maintenance or just support for performance or operational problems?

- Communication. How will you contact the vendor? Will you be able to call, email, and chat? How soon can you expect a response?
- Items to be serviced. Which items will be covered by the SLA? Are there items the contractor will not fix? Is the company contracting to work only on the library computers? Only on the 3-D printer? Will the contractor support your peripherals or software? The items to be covered should be specifically identified in the contract and communicated to the library staff.
- Billing. Will you be charged by the hour, or is there a flat monthly fee? If by the hour, does the contractor charge for a minimum number of minutes or hours a month? Alternatively, is billing based on the particular problem or issue addressed? Will you be billed for the technician's travel time and expenses? Understand what is included and what may incur an additional fee.
- Turnaround. When the library submits a request for service, how soon will support be provided?
- Hours. What days and times will the contractor's staff be available? Will they work on evenings, weekends, or holidays? If so, is there an extra charge for this service?
- Term. What period of time will the agreement cover? What are the procedures for renewing or terminating the agreement?
- Firm agreements are the key to thriving relationships with third-party vendors.

Succession Planning

Staff will leave. This is a fact of life and something that must be addressed in a library's technology plan. Whether the reason for departure is retirement, promotion, a new job, illness, or dismissal, employees will leave. In each of these scenarios, it's important to have a plan that considers staff changes and that includes a way to transfer knowledge.

Most of us have started a job where the person who held the position previously left no documentation or other records. Not only is this frustrating, but also it makes learning the job difficult and time consuming. It can also lead to serious issues with technology updates and even to problems with billing and service coverage. For example, perhaps library employee Mary set up the account for Adobe; updates and billing information are sent to Mary's email address. What happens when Mary no longer works at the library? If notices from Adobe aren't received, critical updates may be missed. If billing invoices are not paid, access and service can lapse.

Establish a procedure that reminds you to change account information when a staff member leaves the library. If your documentation is up to date, it is easy to identify what needs to be revised. To help ensure the transfer of essential knowledge, document critical information as a part of implementing any new technology. Library administrators will need to determine who should keep this documentation and who should have access to it. Documentation for each device should include the following:

- Administrative access. Explain how to access administrative screens of software; this may include specific URLs, user names, passwords, and pin numbers. If the account uses a shared email account, make sure the passwords and pins are changed when staff members leave.
- Maintenance contract details. What is the warranty on each item of technology? What is included in its maintenance contract? If your library paid for an extended warranty or support period, that information needs to be passed on to the person who assumes responsibility for the item.
- Support contacts. Who do you contact to request support for a specific item? Having the contact information kept up to date and in a centralized location can speed the process of resolving a technical issue. Often maintenance contracts for hardware include an elevated level of support, so it is important to know what the contract covers and how to access the elevated support if that has been purchased.
- Maintenance schedules. As discussed earlier in this chapter, regular maintenance is essential to prevent problems with hardware. What needs to be done to maintain each piece of equipment? When is this to be done? Each task should be listed and its completion documented to make sure the work is performed as scheduled. If not, these tasks can be forgotten with staff changes, leading to otherwise avoidable hardware issues.

FINAL THOUGHTS

Planning for maintenance is critical to the success of your technologies. It is important to understand the time needed for maintenance as well as the value of updating and maintaining any technology. Taking the time to clean and perform general maintenance on hardware will extend the lifetime of these new technologies. If you do not plan for maintenance, it will not happen. The result will be an increasing number of technical issues, more downtime, and a lag in version updates.

A comprehensive maintenance plan can lead to higher rates of overall user satisfaction and a greater likelihood that any new equipment will be well used.

Chapter Nine

Ongoing Evaluation and Reporting

In chapter 3, we discussed formulating goals and outcomes for the technology used in your library. As you worked through that process, you thought about the community needs that the library should address, how technology could help meet those needs, and how technology would help the library achieve its overall goals. In chapter 9, we take an in-depth look at the effects of the now-implemented technology and related services to determine whether they are succeeding in reaching those goals and outcomes.

STATISTICS AND EVALUATION

Gathering Statistics

Collecting data regularly may seem daunting, but it is an important step and one that is critical for effective evaluation. Data on the use of equipment and software can help you get the maximum benefit from limited funds. Data can also help you understand the larger picture of usage within your library, making it possible to identify trends before they become problems.

Statistical information can be acquired manually or through automated processes. If at all possible, use automated functions to collect data. Manual collection methods (such as making hash marks on a clipboard at the reference desk) can make the job much more labor intensive, and such methods are often less accurate than information that is collected automatically.

As you purchase, install, and implement new technologies, it is critical to take the time necessary to figure out the following:

- What analytics do you need from the technology? Do you need to know the number of sessions? How long the sessions lasted? What applications were accessed? For the 3-D printer, do you need to know how many hours the printer was used in a month?

- How can this information be collected? Finding out how to access data is vital to ensure statistics are collected properly. It's important to do a test run in the first days after a technology item has been installed. Find out how to get the data needed. For example, is it necessary to run a report from the 3-D printer itself, or do you need to generate a report on the software vendor's website? Establishing the procedure and making sure it works correctly will save you a lot of headaches down the line. The earlier you identify and correct any issues with data collection, the easier it will be to maintain statistics.

Before implementing new technology, determine what data will be needed to make informed decisions in the future and how that data will be collected. Then implement data collection methods at the same time the technology is launched.

It's important to collect data regularly. Failing to do so usually means you will be unable to capture all the data needed; it can be difficult, sometimes even impossible, to re-create statistics that weren't captured at the time of use. If you are proactive in setting up data collection, though, you are more likely to capture all the vital data you need instead of struggling later to fill in blanks where you should have valuable information.

Some technologies lend themselves to easy data collection or have a simple methodology you can deploy. Here are some examples of technical resources that can be used to auto-collect data:

- Firewalls. Firewalls are the hardware and software that determine which users may access which parts of your network. This resource can also provide information about how the network is used, including data on bandwidth usage, numbers of users, and peak times of usage.
- Public computers. If you use an automated reservation system for public computers, that system can supply information about the number of people who use it. Centralized management software can help ascertain which programs are used during each user session. The data can help you determine whether specialized software is being accessed by users and whether computers set aside for specialized functions are being used for those functions. For example, the answers can tell you whether people are using the podcast station to record, edit, or publish podcasts, or whether they're using the stations for some other purpose.
- Vendors. Vendors should be able to supply you with usage data about their products or help you determine how to extract the data you need. As part of your evaluation, look at the data the vendors collect. How can you access this data? Can you get additional information if needed? Weigh the

ease of data collection as an evaluation point when selecting new vendors or equipment.

- Technology checkouts. If you are using the library's circulation system as a theft deterrent by checking out smaller, portable technology items, you already have a built-in method for tracking use. In chapter 8 we discussed circulating small, in-house technologies such as Ozobots, LittleBits, and gaming remotes. This method not only reduces loss due to theft but also has the added benefit of providing easy access to usage statistics through the library's regular circulation reports.
- Hardware. Some larger items of technology—such as 3-D printers and certain other printers—usually record the number of prints and the amount of time the equipment has been used. This information is tracked for maintenance purposes, but the numbers can also help in evaluating usage.
- Door counters. If a technology item is housed in a special room or area with limited access, a simple door counter can help track the number of people entering the area and thereby provide a general idea of usage. Typically, such numbers are only estimates because totals must be adjusted to account for staff movement in and out of the area.

If automating data collection is not possible, tracking usage manually is an option. This creates more work for frontline staff because data must be both recorded and then collated into a meaningful report. If you are faced with manual collection, it might be feasible to gather statistics by sampling rather than recording each activity every day. Sampling can also be done by periodically interviewing users. In addition, it's possible to request self-reporting by users. For example, as people leave the makerspace or finish their activities, you can ask which technologies they used or request that they fill out a brief survey form. If staff members explain to the public that the data will help determine the need for technology and may help justify additional funding, most users will be happy to oblige.

Evaluating User Satisfaction

While gathering statistics is a fundamental aspect of evaluation, statistics alone don't provide all the answers we need. Statistics alone cannot answer such questions as, Is the technology serving its intended purpose? Did users get the results they needed? How can we make technology of this type more useful to library visitors? To answer these questions, you will need more in-depth evaluation techniques.

It's important to answer this fundamental question: did users get what they needed? To find out, don't rely solely on reports from frontline staff. While anecdotes and stories about users can bring the data to life, those anecdotes need to fit into a larger picture. That picture should show how technologies in the library are being used. A story about how a small business owner developed her website, created a marketing campaign, and printed 3-D prototypes in the library can enliven usage statistics on public computers and the 3-D printer. Relating the story of a community member who found a job with help from the library's specialized job resources can help humanize data about workshops and computer usage. However, if you draw a conclusion based on one person's experience or just a single anecdote, it's easy to miss the larger story. As noted previously, the library staff often hears only from a small portion of library users. Many times, those are individuals who needed some type of assistance with the technology. In relying solely on stories about these people, you may miss feedback from a larger user group, including those who worked independently, without interacting with the staff or asking for help.

How, then, do you capture this larger story? Libraries frequently use surveys, focus groups, and interviews to obtain information about users' experiences and points of view. These are the same data collection techniques that were defined and discussed in chapter 2, in the section "Gathering Input from Your Community." This section described the use of surveys, focus groups, and individual interviews to help determine community needs, a vital step in beginning your planning process. These techniques should also be used on a regular basis to determine whether the library's programs, services, and technology are continuing on the right track.

There are several effective methods for surveying users to obtain ongoing feedback. You may find a combination of methods is the most efficient for you or may choose one method that works best with the overall flow of your library.

• Short surveys on specific devices. A useful, short survey can simply ask, "What was your main purpose in coming to the library today?" or, "Did you get what you needed?" These questions can be set to auto-display on public computers, kiosks located near exit doors, or tablets that librarians can hand to users as they finish with a technology. When using this survey method, provide multiple choices for answers and be sure to include an "other" option where people can provide detail in free text. It's also a good idea to allow users to opt out, if they desire. If the short survey is a pop-up on a computer screen, people should be able to decline the survey or to move past the survey page without completing it. Short, quick surveys like these will not provide the same comprehensive picture that more formal surveys can deliver, but they will give you a fast snapshot. Also, short surveys typically have higher response rates than more detailed, in-depth surveys.
• In-depth surveys. Longer, more detailed surveys can be highly effective when you use the tips in chapter 2 to create useful questions. Administer

the survey to the user group or to groups who will have the experience needed to provide the information you seek. Ask only about what you really need to know; omit any nonessential questions. For example, if you want to analyze the use of podcast stations, that survey should target the podcast station users and should ask only about the podcast stations. For maximum effectiveness, in-depth surveys should be conducted digitally and offer an opt-in scenario so that people can choose to participate. Users should be able to go to a kiosk, click on a link on your website or in an email, or otherwise take the survey voluntarily. Surveys should not be administered through a pop-up on a computer screen, and it should not be necessary to complete the survey before using a technology; either of these techniques risks annoying or frustrating respondents.

- Feedback area. It's always valuable to give users opportunities to express appreciation for a useful library service or to suggest improvements. These opportunities can be in digital format or in a traditional paper-and-pencil form deposited in a suggestion box located in the library. Providing a mechanism for constant feedback via your website or public computers also invites frequent input from users.

Surveys, focus groups, and interviews can all be useful and can add layers of anecdotal information to the dry data collected through analytics. Regardless of the methods used, though, it's important to act on the data. Nobody likes to have their opinion solicited and to provide feedback, only to feel their input was ignored. It's not enough to simply ask users if they are reaching their goals on a specific device, whether the hours are convenient, or if they have additional needs; it's important to let those users feel their voices have been heard and that their views matter.

To ensure that users know their comments have been considered, use a public process for evaluating feedback and survey results. This is important even when you're unable to implement changes that users have requested. Displaying a summary of survey results helps users understand where their feedback falls in the big picture of planning for the library's technology services. Providing a response demonstrates that library management is paying attention to users. When changes are made in response to user suggestions, be sure to promote the changes widely, explaining that they were made as a result of public input. If a requested change isn't possible—perhaps due to limited funds or safety concerns—provide the reason. Even when user comments are negative, responding with a brief, positive explanation can be an effective public relations technique.

ANALYZING THE DATA

As you gather analytics and user feedback, you need to schedule time to organize and analyze that data and to create reports. Data reporting can be time consuming, but it's often straightforward if you have a system in place to collect the data and know the reports that need to be created.

Collecting data is important for your own insight and planning, but it may also be a requirement of a grant funder, your parent institution, a regional consortia, or the state library agency. Even if collecting statistics is not required, you need to know how and when the library's services are used. As the saying goes, "If you can't count it, you can't manage it."

Libraries that receive funds through grants or allocations from government agencies are likely to face specific reporting instructions that outline what data is required and when it is to be submitted. Funding—whether from states, cities, or other organizations—that is earmarked for specific projects usually comes with reporting requirements and firm deadlines. Missing a reporting deadline may put your funds in jeopardy—either immediately or for the future. The importance of complying cannot be stressed too much. Make sure you schedule time in your work flow to satisfy these requirements.

A regular pattern of data collection provides established intervals in which to analyze data and identify trends before issues arise. Reviewing data on a systematic basis will allow the library staff to continue to be proactive, rather than reactive. Usage statistics should be reviewed monthly. Someone should be designated to perform this review and to report any anomalies. It's even better to review statistics as a team.

If the formal evaluation is done by a small team or department such as IT or administration, it is vital that the results are shared with all staff members. This enables frontline employees, managers, the IT staff, and everyone else to understand how the library's resources are being used. They can also see how that usage changes over time and in accordance with seasons, community activities, promotion of library services, and other factors. Shared knowledge about library usage can help you make better decisions as a team. Sharing with the staff can be done easily in any of several ways. Some options include the following:

- Forwarding reports to all staff members via email
- Posting statistics on shared drives or a staff intranet. If you choose this method, send a notification email with the link and an announcement when new statistics are posted.
- Displaying charts and other visuals in staff areas
- Distributing statistics in paper form at staff meetings or directly to the staff. If there are some staff members without email, you may need to rely

on paper, but consider providing all staff members with email; it can help with communication in even the smallest libraries.

Distributing statistics to the staff should not be a one-way street. It is not enough just to share the statistics; the distribution method needs to encourage feedback from the staff as well. Shared statistics should be an invitation for discussion. Keep in mind that the IT staff or administrators may not be privy to unanticipated changes or other factors affecting usage that are familiar to frontline staff members who interact with the public.

When analyzing statistics, be on the lookout for the following:

- Spikes in usage. Can you identify a specific reason that an item of technology is suddenly being used more often than in previous months or years? Were there changes in marketing or promotion? Was the technology moved to a different location? Did you recently conduct staff or user training? Was a group, class, or other event scheduled to use the equipment?
- Large dips in usage. If few people have used an item of technology, can you pinpoint a reason? If the amount of usage has declined, can you find out why? Was equipment unavailable due to maintenance issues? Can the maintenance schedule be adjusted to reduce downtime in the future? Was there a change in staff or staffing hours? Should other employees be trained so they can provide coverage for additional hours and assist users if a key staff member is away? Was the library open fewer hours due to a natural disaster or other outside factors? Were there events—either in the library or the community—that distracted the staff or users from focusing on the technology?
- Trends over time. When comparing activity month by month and year to year, what are the long-term trends? Is the use of a particular item of technology slowly declining? If so, why? Is the technology aging? Are newer technologies in greater demand? On the other hand, is usage trending upward? Observing trends over a longer period of time can help you plan better for the future.

Each of these questions should be asked regularly as a part of reviewing statistical data. Moreover, it's not enough to just ask the questions; it's important for your library to respond in a way that will maximize services for users. Perhaps you spot a dip in the usage of job-training computers. Maybe the podcast station or the makerspace has not been used as much recently. These drops may be just seasonal declines related to the school cycle, holidays, or the migration of seasonal residents, but they may also point to a larger issue that should be addressed. For example, by comparing hourly usage fluctuation with staff desk schedules, you might notice that whenever the most tech-savvy children's librarian is not at the desk, there is an overall decline in the usage of children's technologies. An observation like this may point to the need to increase training for other staff members. Perhaps you notice a rising level of usage on the job-training computers. This trend could be due to layoffs or threats of downsizing from a local company with the result that new users are coming into the library to look for employment or to improve their skills. Perhaps the needs of these new users will warrant developing additional training or new programs or other services.

Looking at data frequently and reacting to the information it provides are essential in keeping your library relevant to the community it serves. If data is gathered and analyzed only on a quarterly or—even worse—an annual basis, the library will be slower to react to emerging issues. Small problems that are not addressed can become much larger concerns and can cost a higher price in the quality of user experience, in staff time and in money. Any underutilized resources, especially expensive databases and new technologies, need to be identified and evaluated as early as possible.

To determine the reasons some resources may be underutilized, the library staff will need to play detective and to answer the question *Why?* There may be a single answer or a combination of several factors that need to be addressed.

Training

Are staff members and users comfortable with the technology? Can they use it competently? This is especially important for staff members; if they are unfamiliar with an item or uncomfortable when using it, they will push users to other resources—consciously or unconsciously. They may even forget about the technology. When this is the situation, additional training and hands-on time with the technology can help reverse a trend of low usage.

Maintenance

Are there more technical issues or maintenance requirements than expected? If the technology is not meeting the demands placed on it by your library, analyze the problem. Would regular preventive maintenance head off problems?

Is it possible to revise the work flow to ensure that maintenance service for the device is not performed during open hours? If the device consistently malfunctions, can it be returned or replaced under the maintenance contract or warranty? Here are some additional work flow adjustments to consider:

- Can battery-powered devices be charged overnight?
- Should the 3-D printer be cleaned more often?

• Is it possible to run computer updates after hours?

Identifying developing issues quickly and correcting them can also make a difference when it comes to the maintenance service provided by outside vendors. If maintenance for a device is managed by a commercial company or a department outside the library, the reduced amount of availability and subsequent dips in usage due to technical issues can be a breach of service if the contractor is not responding as the agreement specifies.

Audience

Were your initial plans and intentions for the technology reflected in the data? Is the audience you expected to use the technology actually the group that uses it most? Perhaps you purchased Ozobots or Spheros to teach computer programming to teens. Are teens the ones using these devices most frequently, or are they actually being used by people who are younger or older?

If the outcome achieved by the implementation of technology is different from the initial goal, are changes needed? Should your expectations regarding the use of the equipment be revised to focus on a different demographic group? Would a different approach be more effective in engaging the intended audience? Is a technology you expected to be always available actually limited to staff- or volunteer-conducted programs only? Information on demographics may be collected through surveys of the use of a specific technology and through staff observations. You will need to determine why the access to technology is being limited. For example, does the technology require more staff guidance than expected, or is there a problem with theft? You need to investigate and to determine whether this is a solvable problem.

Location

Is the device located in the best possible place within the library? Is it easy to find, hidden from view, or hard to reach? A place that seemed ideal at first may actually have created a hiding place with the result that the technology is underutilized. Is the device located in a part of the library that is not frequented by the group it was intended to serve? As an example, sometimes a new technology item was placed in the children's area when it would be better suited for teens or adults, or vice versa.

Marketing

How effective is the marketing that has been used to promote the technology? Does it reach the intended users? If not, what needs to change? Would a different message or a different method do a better job of reaching the intended audience?

In summary, for both successfully used technologies and those that are underutilized, it is important to look at changes in statistics as well as user feedback to determine the reasons for usage patterns.

ARE YOU MEETING YOUR GOALS?

When studying usage data and community input, the fundamental question to ask is, Are you meeting your goals? Chapter 3 explained the process of assessing the library's technology and determining community needs. Now you've chosen and installed new technology to meet those needs. After using it a while, it's important to take a step back and look at the big picture of how that technology is supporting your library's mission.

It's easy to get bogged down in statistics and user feedback, but these resources are not the endgame. They are only tools to use in your quest to achieve the goals and outcomes outlined for your library. As an example, let's revisit a possible goal discussed in chapter 3. One such goal was *Provide support to Unity Library's small business community.* Among the reasonable outcomes selected to support this goal were (1) Configure and utilize the router to maximize bandwidth; and (2) Provide job retraining opportunities.

To determine whether you're meeting the overarching goal—that of supporting small businesses—you will need both statistics and user feedback. Use the data collected to explain how this goal is being met through specific outputs and how you will continue to grow your success in pursuing this goal. For example, you may state the number of job-training stations and the number of coding classes and other related programming. In addition, you will want to identify improvements made to the infrastructure to manage new resources and to serve more users; the amount of increased bandwidth gained is a specific, measurable result. When relating a measurement such as bandwidth, place it in context; explain how many additional simultaneous users can be accommodated and what other resources are supported by the increased bandwidth. As you reflect, you'll spot opportunities to further expand the library's support for the business community and how existing resources can be used to continue focusing on the goal of helping the small business community.

CREATING STATISTICAL REPORTS

Libraries are often required to submit reports on equipment usage as well as data on other programs and services. This information is frequently required by grantors, local government, or other agencies providing financial support.

At a minimum, the person charged with collecting statistical data needs to be proficient with spreadsheet software such as Microsoft Excel, Apple's Numbers, or Google Spreadsheet. However, the ability to simply input or list numbers isn't enough. Those responsible for statistics also need to be able to manipulate the data to generate totals, create basic tables, and prepare reports that can be understood by everyone. Tools like MySQL and the advanced functionality within software like Excel can really help the staff to flesh out statistics. If those selected to gather statistics lack a strong knowledge of these tools, identify training opportunities within the library, the local college, the library consortia, or other source where they can increase their skill. Without this knowledge, they will spend much more time than necessary bringing data together, creating unnecessary work for themselves, and likely producing final reports containing errors.

The data collected for these reports may be in the form of raw numbers and, as such, can be meaningless without context. Reports need to help tell the story of the technology, not just cite numbers. Providing context, especially by telling stories, can add human faces to the numbers. In addition, a report that is visually appealing and well organized can achieve a greater impact than just numbers alone. Therefore, it is important to develop a strategy for combining the numbers, anecdotes, and user survey information into a cohesive document.

In today's culture, every dollar earmarked for your library's specific project could just as easily be used by a different organization for a different project. There is fierce competition for funds from public and private grantmakers and from state and local governments. There is also competition among schools and between branches or departments of public libraries. Submitting a report gives you an opportunity to explain the good that you are accomplishing. It's also an opportunity to persuade decision makers that the technologies described in the report really matter and are making a difference in achieving the purpose for which the funds were supplied. Equally important, if your project is not achieving the expected results, the report should indicate what has happened and why, and should suggest a plan for going forward. Correcting the path of a project early on can turn a failure into a success.

The key to effective reporting is to provide readers with the information they require in the clearest, most accurate format. Often those reading your reports must read multiple grant or departmental reports; they won't have the time to decipher the meaning hidden between lines of numbers or to hunt through your report to understand its implications.

Visualizing Data

Depicting data visually is a highly effective way to use otherwise dull data to tell an engaging story. Charts and graphs are an easy way to compare services, technologies, and resources that are being used with those that are not being well used.

There are multiple resources for creating visual displays of data or for creating infographics to illustrate information. Visual reports can create easily digestible documents for publication; such documents can capture the attention of people who generally skim material and help them understand the big picture.

Be especially careful with reports to funders. It is important to understand and provide all the information funders require and to present it in the format they request; in such cases, use visual displays to highlight specific statistics or facts and to supplement longer narratives or statistical tables. In writing grant reports, it is advisable to use bullets, graphics, and succinct phrasing to provide a clear picture of the salient details. Use the text to support your main points.

Online resources for the visualization of data include the following:

The Data Visualisation Catalogue (http://datavizcatalogue.com)

This free site explains which types of charts are most appropriate for displaying different types of data. It also lists tools, many of which are free, that can be used to generate the desired graphic.

Google GIF Maker (http://datagifmaker.withgoogle.com)

This animated GIF maker, a tool for creating visual data for library websites, will allow you to compare two resources. The data collected can be used as an embedded feature in online reports or as a statistical display on a website.

Tableau (http://www.tableau.com)

Tableau is a software solution for creating colorful and unique graphic views of data as well as graphic representations that combine multiple data sets. For libraries that work with large amounts of data, this may be a useful tool to help show a broad picture. For example, by using Tableau, a library's data on technology use, circulation, door counts, and programming statistics can be displayed in a single integrated chart. This can help the staff, funders, and the public understand how various aspects are related overall, a perspective that can be lost when focusing analysis on just one area, statistic, or library service. In addition, the software includes links to data sources so that reports are automatically updated as new data is available. Figure 9.1 is an example of the use of Tableau to illustrate makerspace usage; a full-color version of this image can be seen at https://goo.gl/4UB2HZ. Although this software must be purchased, Tableau can sometimes be found at a discounted price on TechSoup, an organization that provides technology resources to libraries and other nonprofits. Also, small nonprofits may apply to Tableau directly for a donated license; schools, colleges, and government agencies are ineligible for this donation.

ICIMO and LibPAS

ICIMO (http://www.icimo.com) and LibPAS (http://countingopinions.com) are subscription database data aggregators specifically created for the library community. They help bring together multiple data points and generate in-depth reports on your library services and technology usage.

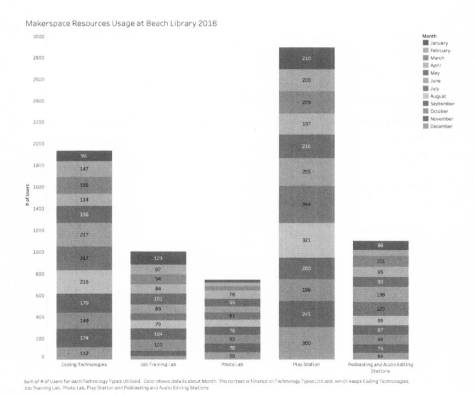

Figure 9.1.   Example of makerspace resource usage created using Tableau

Piktochart (http://piktochart.com)

Piktochart is a free resource for creating infographics and is especially useful for those who lack graphic design experience. Colorful, eye-catching infographics can explain your technology usage and progress toward goals or other library stories in visually striking ways. Infographics can be used to help summarize a long report and can show the highlights of your report in a memorable manner.

Figure 9.2 is a small infographic developed using Piktochart; a full-color version of this image can be seen at https://goo.gl/v4DqSG. An infographic like this can be used to help people understand quickly how the community uses the library's makerspace. The infographic also illustrates which resources are used each month.

These visual tools can be used in multiple ways. An infographic or other visualization of data can be used as a summary statement that is part of a larger document. Embedded within a web page, these displays can provide dynamic data or animated charts. In printed form, visualizations can be in-

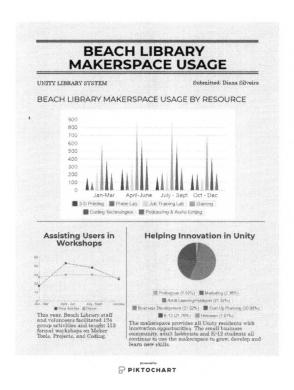

Figure 9.2.   Infographic displaying Beach Library's makerspace usage

cluded in a handout for budget meetings or distributed to other specific groups.

FINAL THOUGHTS

Regularly evaluating and applying lessons learned from the data you collect helps ensure that your library will be more responsive to the needs of its community. On the other hand, if you neglect to collect statistics and user feedback or ignore the results, your library will miss the mark in delivering services to the people it aims to serve.

Chapter Ten

Planning for the Future

MAKING THE MOST OF YOUR TECHNOLOGY PLAN

Throughout the process of researching community and library technology needs, developing goals and plans to address those needs, and implementing effective technologies for your library, success depends on keeping your technology plan in the forefront. If you merely develop the plan and file the document away, success may never be achieved. Instead, your library is likely to fall into its same old patterns where technology purchases are made in reaction to crises rather than based on decisions that arise from clear goals, a defined purpose, and carefully selected outcomes.

Even more than a guide for purchases and implementation, the technology plan should be a resource that's revisited regularly; frequent checkups will ensure that library services move forward with updated and newer technologies to meet evolving needs. Six-month periods are reasonable intervals for looking closely at the technology plan and for determining how each step is progressing. At these intervals, review how well the realities of purchasing, implementing, and training are stacking up against the initial plan. This review should look at four important areas: the implementation schedule, the budget, unexpected technical issues that have emerged, and the successes and failures that have occurred.

Implementation Schedule

Is implementation of the plan proceeding as anticipated? Have tasks been completed as planned? Is the overall process of implementation proceeding at the rate you expected?

Your technology plan likely included both smaller projects and large-scale, multipart implementations; evaluate each of these, both individually and as part of the larger plan. Look at each project element to ensure work has been completed or is likely to be completed as scheduled.

As an example of a small-scale project, perhaps you planned to evaluate router settings and to implement different settings for increased security. Another small-scale project may have been to update all computers to the new operating system. Were these tasks completed? Smaller projects like these can often have a major impact on current technology; for this reason, they need to be completed before larger projects are initiated. Although they may not seem as exciting as introducing brand-new technologies like podcast stations or makerspaces, these smaller, basic technology improvements are just as vital for the success of the library's technology services. Therefore, ensure that implementation timelines for all project elements keep on schedule.

When you notice that some aspect of an implementation has fallen behind the planned timeline, determine the reason. This may require doing some research and asking questions. Was there a delay in receiving funding, in arranging for construction, or in fulfillment of the order by the vendor? On the other hand, was the issue an in-house problem, such as a lack of staff time to set up, install, and deploy the new technology? While hiccups in the process will inevitably happen, it's important to determine whether the implementation issue is symptomatic of a larger issue within the library. If there is an ongoing issue and it's not corrected, additional delays are likely in the future.

Budget

Were funds for technology purchases allocated and made available in the way and at the time you anticipated? If you were counting on grant funds, was the grant only partially funded, or was the original project budget reduced?

If the amount of funding originally expected was cut, the technology plan may need to be adjusted. Failing to reevaluate priorities and simply continuing to spend until the money runs out—and then stopping—is not recommended as a best practice. Instead, step back and reconsider the technology plan. If possible, rather than forging ahead to implement a new service or technology, reallocate available funding to higher-priority technology needs or focus on keeping current technology functional. Keep in mind that, if you're working with grant funds or if the technology is to be purchased with specifically earmarked funds, you may need to obtain approval first from the grantor before making such changes; without such approval, reallocating funds for different purposes might not be possible. Some grant providers, when announcing a reduced level of funds, may ask you to submit a revised budget and action plan for approval before any expenditures are made.

Unexpected Technical Issues

While reviewing the technology plan and your implementation timeline, reflect on any problems you have encountered. Were these issues fully resolved, or will the same issues continue to cause turmoil and delays as you progress through your plan? For example, did staff members have adequate time to set up technology? If the lack of sufficient time was a problem, was there a onetime issue that required staff attention, or did the press of regular duties demand all their attention? If the latter, what has been done to free work schedules so staff members will have sufficient time for technology implementation and training in the future?

On the other hand, did you find issues with the technology itself? For example, was there insufficient bandwidth to accommodate additional devices? Were there problems with wireless connectivity when installing a new makerspace area? Did the firewall settings within the library building interfere with implementing a new software program?

How were problems handled? For the sake of moving forward, was a quick fix deployed to temporarily remedy the situation, or did you create a long-term solution? For example, if there were human resource issues, what was the nature of the problem and how was it addressed? Was there a need to begin earlier to recruit and train a sufficient number of volunteers? Should staff time have been reallocated? Would it have been better to bring in a third party to provide training or maintenance? Have those problems been solved?

With technical issues, make sure you understand all the components that contributed to the problem. This is an especially important component of problem solving when any part of your IT support is provided by those who are not on library premises or part of the library staff. Some libraries depend on system-wide settings that are managed by IT personnel at the county, city, or school district level. In such cases, it's essential to have early and careful planning for seamless implementation of technology. When changes to settings on equipment are necessary, the process often involves multiple steps and communication. Therefore, once you believe you've found the solution, it's key that you test and update those settings as part of the implementation. Document the change to ensure the setting stays changed or can be made in the future. For example, some software requires that special ports are open; these may be ports that IT managers normally keep closed. When this occurs, the library staff needs to document the specific port and the reason the setting needed to be changed.

As a case study, look at the experience of Unity Library where the library's firewall is maintained by the county IT department. The library's new technology services were affected when its cloud-based server for website hosting was changed. The server's internal settings related to the library's firewall and to vendor settings needed to be modified before authentication could be completed and access could continue. The Internet Protocol (IP) address and server details were not communicated to outside vendors or to the county IT department in a timely fashion; therefore, the library's website and several online resources were inaccessible within the library and to remote users until the problem was resolved.

While you move forward with the rest of the technology plan, make sure you document and build upon the knowledge you have gained with each step; bring that knowledge into the plan. The staff members of Unity Library have added a further step to their technology plan based on their experience with the website server and the county IT department. The library's plan now specifies that, in the future, any changes that involve new IP addresses are to include instructions about distributing those addresses to appropriate vendors and other designated contacts.

Successes and Failures

As you evaluate your technology plan, remember to remain focused on the goals you identified at the beginning of the process. Are you making progress toward reaching those goals? Which steps have been successful? Where have you missed the mark?

As you revisit and continue with the next phase of your technology plan, use the evaluations you learned to conduct in chapter 9 to help you readjust or change course as needed. If a program, a technology, or even a stated goal is not being met, it is never too late to pause, evaluate, and determine what changes need to be made in order to achieve it.

CREATING THE NEXT PLAN

But wait! I am still working on my current plan. This could be your first thought at the suggestion of developing a new plan. It may be true that you're still working on implementing the first plan. In reality, though, by the time you are midway through the current plan, it's time to start looking at the next planning cycle.

One important part of any technology plan is a provision for how and when work should begin on creating the next plan. Perhaps your current plan is for a three-year period; in this case, you need to have a new plan fully ready before the beginning of year 3 of the current plan. Doing so will create continuity and ensure there are no gaps in your technology planning and implementation. By having the next plan already in place, you will be able to move smoothly from one plan to the next.

Through the process of writing your current plan, you gained a strong understanding of the time needed to create and implement an effective and successful plan. In developing the next plan, you're likely to find that some steps will be easier or more streamlined the second time around. As an example, you will complete the technology audit more easily and much faster if, after the initial audit, you continued to update the inventory with additions, deletions, and reassignments of equipment and other resources as those changes occurred.

Your current technology plan should include a section on creating the next plan. Providing a written guide that explains what needs to happen in the future—regardless of intervening staffing changes at any level—will help make the library more accountable to its funders and to the public. It will also make everyone's work easier.

By following the steps laid out in this book, you and your colleagues will have put together a comprehensive technology plan that includes an audit of technology resources and needs, a description of the steps involved in implementation, and an approach to evaluation—all based on the needs of your community. Your plan should outline the overall process that was used to create the current technology plan, providing a framework for those who will develop the next plan. This section of the document should identify the type of information to be gathered and presented in the plan, along with a basic timeline; these details will provide the foundation to get the next plan started.

Assessing Community Needs

As a way to maintain a community focus for future iterations of your technology planning, consider outlining how community members were involved in creating the original plan. Explain how surveys, focus groups, and interviews were used and how statistics played a role in decision-making related to technology improvements. Also, list outside groups that participated by helping to bring the needs of different user groups to the planning table. Were these participants from other departments within your county or school, or from local schools? Did they include representatives of the chamber of commerce, other civic groups, and community leaders? Listing the groups or individuals who provided input will help those responsible for developing future plans to better understand how needs were identified and priorities determined. As you reflect on the community groups included in the first planning cycle, you may think of new groups that have been established since the first plan was developed or of segments of the community that were not initially involved. In considering the groups that form your community, you may also be able to identify opportunities for partnerships or joint projects in the future.

Over the course of implementing your technology plan, your relationship with library users has changed. The needs that you fill for those users have changed too. With each new service, device, or software that has been added or modified, you had an opportunity to reach out to existing users as well as to new user groups. Hopefully, you've been able to engage both groups in new ways. Those who develop the next version of the plan will need to reflect on the successes and failures of the past plan. How have those successes and failures changed the ways in which the library is used? How has that experience changed the community's expectations of the services the library should provide?

Considering all of this can seem daunting. Fortunately, the current technology plan laid the foundation for this introspection by the new planning committee members. With the evaluation of progress toward the library's primary goals and additional information from statistics that were captured to document technology usage, the committee now has a straightforward process to follow. By using the data collected during each planning phase to plan for the next cycle, the process will run more smoothly and the insights gained can be even more profound.

In writing the plan for the future, assume that no current staff members will be available to guide the planning process. Be specific and detailed in laying out the lessons learned and in providing overall guidance from your recent experience.

Involving the Right People

The completed technology plan should list, by both name and position, the members of the planning committee that created it. In addition, the plan should identify those personnel who are to be responsible for developing and implementing the next plan. Those individuals should be identified only by position because there are likely to be at least some staffing changes over the two to three years covered by the initial plan.

In thinking of whom to include in working on the next plan, reflect on those who served on the current technology planning committee. Was there input from all essential areas of staff, or did you feel you missed a voice? Were all departments, locations, and levels within the library represented? If so, what were the positions held by those representatives? How were those people identified? What should be done differently the next time around?

Timeline

In charting the course for your next technology plan, include a basic timeline. At a minimum, identify the starting date to begin thinking about the next planning phase, and provide a general time frame. This will help the next group of planners balance budget development with an effective approach for upgrading and expanding technology.

Evaluating Experimental Technology for the Future

By indicating a timeline to be followed for developing the next technology plan, you are designating a window in the schedule when the staff can consider long-term technology needs. In the early planning stages of the next plan, you might want to create an opportunity for experimentation, to try out new and upcoming technology trends to see if they have a place within your library.

Having the resources to explore new trends can help shape future technology plans. In the long run, these technologies may be hits or misses as far as meeting needs of your community, but having the library associated with the newest technologies and positioned as a center for users to learn about cutting-edge technology may be part of your long-range plan. To effectively evaluate new, "bleeding edge," or experimental technologies, you need to provide at least some funds in the budget and a framework or guidelines for how this experimentation will take place. Funds may be included in the budget for the next technology plan or may come from other sources.

How will these experimental technologies differ from those in your overall technology plan? For one thing, you might choose to introduce these technologies in a different manner. Instead of being announced as an ongoing service and assigned to a permanent location, these technologies could be considered as pilot programs, betas, or try-out periods. The terms "pilot" or "beta" can refer to small-scale programs created in a specific department or limited to one branch library. If these small-scale trials are successful, they might be rolled out to additional locations or scaled to serve additional users. A new technology could also be introduced as a staff-only resource, one that is initially used only for staff work. In this way the technology could play a role in training and educating staff as well as determining whether and in what ways it might fit into the library's long-range and technology plans. Being careful, responsible, and systematic about planning does not exclude experimentation; it simply requires an approach to experimentation that is thoughtful.

Providing opportunities to experiment with new technology can be one of the most fun and rewarding parts of technology planning. Once library staff members understand experimental technologies, they are better equipped to evaluate whether those technologies will fit the needs of the community and library. Of course, any technology that is considered for full integration within the library must be incorporated into the library's technology plan. This will ensure that maintenance, integration with current services, training, and accountability are anticipated for the technology and that its implementation fits into the overall plan.

One example of a technology some libraries initially deployed as a pilot program is virtual reality. A library might begin by purchasing a HoloLens, a virtual reality headset manufactured by Microsoft. A HoloLens allows users to add virtual interactions like video, real-time communications, images, and information to their real world. This virtual reality setting can enable learning, gaming, and exploration of the world and beyond while people are still in the library building. Libraries are using these devices to teach game development, to transport users to virtual locations, and to communicate with others around the globe.

Before a service such as virtual reality can be rolled out to the public, at least a few staff members must learn to use the device. They must be ready to explain the device effectively and feel comfortable helping users to get the most from it. Once the library staff understands the device's use and potential, the technology can be deployed in a pilot program where it's introduced to users on a limited scale. If the pilot is successful, it's easier to justify the purchase of more devices and the service can be included in the next technology plan.

FINAL THOUGHTS

This stage of the planning process is your chance to make recommendations for the next planning cycle. So be sure to take a step back and evaluate the entire planning process. As you begin thinking about the next technology plan, use what you learned during this process to help make the next planning process even more successful. By building on your experience, you can make the process better, more efficient, and more inclusive for the next time.

Chapter Eleven

Moving Forward with Your Plan

Congratulations! You have completed your first technology plan. As you worked through this book, you likely created your first comprehensive library planning document. This was not an easy task—so take a moment to congratulate yourself on a job well done.

Creating a technology plan is a key part of making your library successful. The technology plan should both work as a stand-alone document with an implementation plan and support the library's overall long-range or strategic plan. While technology may be only one prong of the library's long-term plan, it integrates into almost every aspect of the library. For this reason, the technology plan is vital if the library is to grow and meet the needs of its users.

As we conclude, it is important to reflect on some key takeaways regarding the planning process and on tips for achieving your goals with your technology plan.

- Update regularly. Remember to update your technology inventory whenever you bring new technologies into the library and when you remove outdated software or hardware. The audit created at the beginning of the planning process should be considered a "living document" that reflects the current state of technology within the library at any given time.
- Train staff. Providing the staff with adequate training must always be on the forefront of any technology implementation. Without staff members who understand the uses of a specific technology and who are ready to promote services and help users, implementations will fail. Training is rarely a onetime activity; it should be a continual process that is fully integrated into every staff member's work processes.

- Stay flexible. The technology plan is not written in stone. As you implement the plan, use new information and your professional judgment to ensure success. The best approach may be to shift aspects of the plan in response to developments that occur either inside the library or in your community or school. As you move forward, you may find processes are streamlined, resources are updated, and the skill levels of the staff are improved; any of these can allow acceleration of the timeline at some points. In the larger community, newer technology may be released that fits your needs better, or different initiatives may be launched to meet the newly determined needs of your user base.
- Avoid roadblocks. If there are setbacks that prevent implementation from taking place as scheduled, do not place the plan aside; instead, look for other ways to proceed. For example, if part of the plan is delayed due to budget or construction constraints, revise the plan to accomplish what can be done within the available time frame. While you're waiting for one step to be completed, let another move forward so you can still accomplish your goals.
- Market services. Promoting new technologies, updating existing technology, and generally marketing all the technology services your library has to offer should be an ongoing process. Develop customized messages to help different audiences understand how these resources can benefit them as individuals and as part of the larger community.
- Evaluate constantly. Collecting and analyzing data must be an ongoing process. When you wear many hats, it's easy to let the job of analyzing statistics slide—but it must not! Catching trends early is vital to achieving your goals. You need to know what is working, what needs to be tweaked, and what areas are missing their benchmarks.
- Listen constantly. Actively seeking feedback, especially when it's not positive, can help you find success. Even informal feedback can help you identify issues and find ways to revise your technology plan. Sometimes, a simple off-the-cuff comment can provide information that's just as useful as more formal evaluations. Keep in mind, however, that the comment may represent only a single voice; your library has many users with a variety of perspectives, so weigh changes accordingly.

Planning, implementation, and evaluation are all part of the cycle. As you go through each stage of your technology plan, communicate about developments. Keep the staff, stakeholders, and funders aware of the achievements and milestones your plan has achieved. These accomplishments, the success (or failures) of new technology, and the issues arising while implementing them all need to be public knowledge. Everyone with an interest in the library—the library staff, the library's larger organizational network, city and county officials, and any other stakeholders—need to see how the technology implementation is progressing.

Each enhancement to existing technology, or implementation of a new technology, helps the library evolve. These changes contribute to the library's place in the community today and in the future. As the technology plan is implemented, the services offered will create opportunities for the library to connect to new groups of people, individuals who may not have previously been library users. For example, a makerspace can draw a tech-based crowd, tinkers, or young adults who did not use the library before. Similarly, when you create resources for the small business community, professionals who had not entered the library may begin to use its resources. Whenever a library service touches a new individual, there's an opportunity to connect and to show how valuable the library can be.

Remember that a plan is only as useful as your dedication to implement it and keep it moving. The planning, implementation, and maintenance of technology is never completed. It is important to keep your library from lapsing back into the technical situations you just corrected. Ensure a strong plan by keeping an active and accurate inventory, by training and assisting the staff in learning to use technology, by evaluating the effectiveness of technologies, and most importantly, by maintaining your current technologies through the application of updates, patches, and new versions as needed. The more you stay involved by following the steps explored in this book, the more successful you will be in using technology and in engaging your community through the library's digital resources.

It is my utmost hope that this book has provided the resources, the advice, and the guidance to help your library create a strong technology plan and to achieve success with your technology and long-term goals.

I welcome your suggestions and questions. Please reach out and let me know how your library fared through the planning process. I can be contacted via email at diana@novarelibrary.com.

Appendix

Indiana Public Library Technology Plan Template

As of January 1, 2011, public libraries in Indiana are required to follow the standards in 590 IAC 6 in order to be eligible for the receipt of state and federal funds. These standards require that public libraries report bylaws and long-range and technology plans to the Indiana State Library. This template and its accompanying documents are designed to help public libraries in meeting the reporting requirements outlined in the standards.

THE PLANNING PROCESS

The Indiana State Library does not indicate a planning process that a public library must use to develop its long-range or technology plans. However, elements of best practices are demonstrated in the templates. These templates are provided in order to give a basic structure to those libraries that may need some guidance in this area.

INDIANA STATE LIBRARY TEMPLATES

Public libraries are welcome to design long-range and technology plans that do not use the provided templates. In this case, it is recommended to use the included checklist to ensure all requirements are met.

A template for library board bylaws is also available.

WHAT'S INSIDE

The template packet includes the following items:

- Checklist. Already have a plan and need to check it against the standards? Use the checklist to make sure you've included all of the requirements.
- Template. A simple document that arranges content as outlined in the standards. Use the template if you need a format to use that's acceptable in reporting your plan to the Indiana State Library. Examples are included to help get you started.
- Instructions. Detailed instructions on how to complete the template. Use the instructions for help in completing the template document included.

TECHNOLOGY PLAN TEMPLATE

The instructions explain both the required elements and the tools used to write particular parts of the plan, as indicated below.

- Goals and realistic strategies. Defines the technology goals for the library within the years covered by the plan, as well as the realistic strategies (i.e., objectives) set to reach them.
- Professional development strategy. Outlines the library's plan to provide the staff with the skills needed to achieve its technology goals.
- Assessment of technology resources (form). Inventories the library's current or desired technology resources and whether or not improvements are needed.
- Equipment replacement schedule (form). Provides a schedule to replace outdated technology resources for each year of the plan.
- Financial resources (form). Indicates a budget for each year of the plan, including which funds will be used to cover expenditures for technology resources.
- Evaluation. Describes how the plan will be evaluated against the goals and realistic strategies it contains.
- Automation plan. Includes the library's plan to automate, or its plan to maintain an existing integrated library system (ILS).

Other sections may be added as required to address unique local circumstances or to elaborate on a library's efforts to provide technology resources to its patrons.

The conventions in the figure below are used throughout the sample plan document.

Text Style	Definition
Plain	This text is optional.
Italics	This text is suggested.
Bold	This text is required by standards, statute, or both.
[BRACKETED]	This is text to be filled in by the user.
<u>Underlined</u>	This text is informational or provides instructions.

FORMS

There are forms in the template that require the library to examine the resources it has to achieve its goals. An evaluation form is included as an example, but it is optional. Detailed instructions for filling out all forms are also included.

- Assessment of Technology Resources. This form suggests libraries take an inventory of those resources and services that are provided to the public. Simply check a box as to whether or not the resource or service complies with public library standards. Libraries may also indicate if a resource or service is provided based on a specific community need.
- Financial Resources. This form becomes the budget for the library's long-range plan. Complete one for each year of the plan, showing how resources or services that have been assessed will be funded. Just enter the dollar amount in the appropriate box on the form.
- Evaluation (optional form). The brief evaluation form included uses a sample goal from the template. The library may choose to develop other evaluation forms or methods that are appropriate to its local environment. Use the included form to help you get started.

TECHNOLOGY PLAN CHECKLIST
FOR INDIANA PUBLIC LIBRARY STANDARDS

In order to be in compliance with Indiana Public Library standards (590 IAC 6-1-4(g)), use the checklist below to ensure the following elements are included in your submission to the Indiana State Library.

Keep in mind that this template covers only what is required by the public library standards. You may need to consult other resources for further information. See the Library Development Office website for a list: http://www.in.gov/library/ldoresources.htm

Does the technology plan . . .	Yes
Cover, at most, three years?	☐
List the library goals and realistic strategies for using telecommunications and information technology to respond to needs of the community?	☐
Provide a professional development strategy to ensure the staff has the skills and training necessary to meet the library's technology goals?	☐
Assess the library's current telecommunication services, hardware, software, and other services that comply with basic standards for the population served by the library?	☐
Indicate a replacement schedule for telecommunication services, hardware, software, and other services to meet continuing needs of the community?	☐
Include a budget for the costs of telecommunication services, hardware, software, and other services required during the years covered by the plan?	☐
Describe the ongoing annual evaluation of the plan's goals and strategies that includes revision and modifications filed with the Indiana State Library?	☐
Outline the library's automation plan that indicates the library's collections are managed through the use of an integrated library system (ILS)?	☐

Please contact Indiana State Library, Library Development Office, at ldo@library.IN.gov with any questions you may have.

TECHNOLOGY PLAN TEMPLATE

INSTRUCTIONS

[NAME]

PUBLIC LIBRARY

Three Year Technology Plan

[YEAR] to [YEAR]

[NAME] Public Library Technology Plan Committee

[DATE]

Committee Members:

[LIST NAMES AND AFFILIATIONS OF COMMITTEE MEMBERS]

TECHNOLOGY PLAN TEMPLATE

Goals and Realistic Strategies

The following is sample text you may use to define the library's goals and realistic strategies as they relate to technology resources. Please refer to the instructions for further details.

These goals and strategies represent the library's effort to maintain a technologically rich environment for its residents.

Goal:

Children will be engaged in dynamic and challenging learning opportunities delivered by way of technology.

Realistic Strategy:
In six months the library will add a children's workstation with age-appropriate learning software.

Goal:

Patrons will be able to use self-checkout stations in order to decrease their wait time for routine transactions.

Realistic Strategy:
In the next fiscal year, the library will purchase two self-checkout machines and measure and observe results.

Goal:

Patrons of all ages will find new ways to enjoy cultural and historical resources via the digitization of images, sounds and videos.

Realistic Strategy:
Library staff members will take Indiana State Library digitization classes offered in the first quarter of 20XX and identify items to be digitized within one month of the class.

Professional Development Strategy

The following is sample text you may use to define the library's professional development strategy as it relates to technology resources. Please see the instructions for further details.

The following goals and strategies represent the library's commitment to provide staff members who are knowledgeable about technology concepts and practices.

Goal:

Provide library staff with training for standard office computer applications (e.g., Word, Excel, PowerPoint, etc.) related to in-house usage.

Realistic Strategy:

In the first quarter of 20XX, the IT staff will compose a tutorial for creating a Word document (e.g., an office memorandum) that includes instructions for using fonts, bulleted lists, and paragraph formatting.

Realistic Strategy:

Twice per year, the professional staff will attend a workshop where participants use a standard office application to create a product that is useful to them in their everyday work, such as an Excel worksheet for a program budget.

TECHNOLOGY PLAN TEMPLATE

Assessment of Technology Resources

YEAR: [YEAR]	Currently Have/Need [list telecommunication service, hardware, software, or other service]	Required by Standard [list corresponding standard]	Identified by Community Needs [compliance level will not be used]	Indiana Public Library Standards Compliance Level			
				Basic	Enhanced	Exceptional	Improve
Telecomm. Services							
Main	5 telephones, 1 central line for public	Telephone listed in library's name		X			
	Outgoing message after hours, voicemail on all phones	Voice mail or other method to inform public of hours		X			
	2 T1 lines	Internet connection speed at least 1.5 mbps		X		10 mbps fiber	
Hardware							
Main	Photocopier ($0.10 per b/w copy)	Copier	eBook readers	X			
	Public fax ($1.70 1st pg, $1.00/pg, each add'l)	Fax machine Class C serving 8,736	Digital camera	X			
	Public computer lab (10 workstations)			X			
Branch	Children's literacy workstation	Children's service		X	Wireless Internet		
Software							
	Integrated Library System software	Integrated Library System		X			
Branch	Children's literacy software	Children's service		X			

TECHNOLOGY PLAN TEMPLATE

YEAR: [YEAR]		Required by Standards [list corresponding standard]	Identified by Community Needs [compliance level will not be used]	Indiana Public Library Standards Compliance Level			
Other Services				Basic	Enhanced	Exceptional	Improve
	Reference database		Adult reference service	X			

TECHNOLOGY PLAN TEMPLATE

Equipment Replacement Schedule

	Assessed Resource [list equipment to be replaced]	**[YEAR]**			
		Q1	Q2	Q3	Q4
Telecomm. Services					
Main		NA	NA	NA	NA
Hardware					
Main	Photocopier ($0.10 per b/w copy)	NA	NA	NA	NA
	Public fax ($1.70 1st pg, $1.00/pg, each add'l)			X	
	Public computer lab workstations 1-5		X		
	Public computer lab workstations 6-10				X
Branch	Children's literacy workstation	X			
Software					
Main					
Branch					
Other Services					
Main					
Branch					

TECHNOLOGY PLAN TEMPLATE

Financial Resources

YEAR: [YEAR]	Currently Have/Need [list telecommunication service, hardware, software, or other service]	Operating	Funds LIRF	LCPF	Rainy Day	eRate	Fund 6
Telecomm. Services							
Main	5 telephones, 1 central line for public	$4,500					
	Outgoing message after hours, voicemail on all phones	$0					
	10 mbps fiber	$13,348				$31,145	
	Canon Powershot Digital Camera	$200.00					
Hardware							
Main	Photocopier ($0.10 per b/w copy)	$4,000					
	Public fax ($1.70 1st pg, $1.00/pg, each add'l)	$1,000					
	Public computer lab (10 workstations)			$25,000			
Branch	Children's literacy workstation	$2,400					
	Color Nook (ebook reader)			$250.00			
Software							
	Integrated Library System Vendor Name	$18,000					
Branch	Children's Literacy software for workstation	$0					
Other Services							
	Automotive repair database	$6,000					

Evaluation

The following is sample text you may use to describe the library's evaluation process as it relates to technology resources. Please see the instructions for further details.

This plan will be reviewed at the library board's annual meeting of each year covered by the plan. The assessment and financial resources section will be evaluated at that time and modified accordingly. All revisions will be submitted to the state library within one month of the board's annual meeting.

Certain strategies described above require evaluation more frequently. Quarterly updates during each plan year will be made to the board as to the progress toward those specific objectives.

The table below is a sample Excel form you may use to evaluate a hardware/software goal and strategy. Please see instructions for further details.

Timeframe:		
Library goal:		
Library objective:		
Category	Software	Hardware
Item		
Cost	$0	$0
Purchase Date	mm/dd/yy	mm/dd/yy

Automation Plan

The technology plan is a three-year plan that must include a description of the library's current technological resources, with realistic goals and a strategy for using telecommunications and information technology within their community. Included in this plan is a schedule for equipment replacement and a discussion of the financial and professional development resources available to support this technology. Also within this plan, the library needs to state that it agrees to catalog materials according to a nationally recognized cataloging standard (i.e., Library of Congress, Dewey, NLM, etc.) to fulfill the "automation plan" requirement of 590 IAC 6-1-4 (h)(4)(G).

INSTRUCTIONS

(Technology Plan Template)

As of January 1, 2011, a three-year technology plan for service in public libraries is required by Indiana public library standards (590 IAC 6). Technology planning is an important responsibility of the library board, with input from the director. It is advisable to assign a board committee to manage this process.

These instructions provide the basic information you need to complete the sample plan document that follows. Use the checklist above to ensure all components are included. Please note that the template is designed to result in the submission of the library's technology plan to the Indiana State Library as required by public library standards. Formats for other audiences are left to individual libraries to create and develop.

For technology planning, WebJunction may be used as a resource: http://www.webjunction.org. TechAtlas (http://www.techatlas.org) is also a good resource for understanding measureable goals and realistic technology objectives. The instructions and the template that follow are based on the eRate model outlined in chapter 10 of the "New Director Information" at http://www.in.gov/library/3310.htm.

Title Page

Fill In	Instructions
[NAME]	Insert the library's name where indicated.
[YEAR]	Insert the beginning and ending years that the plan covers.
[DATE]	Enter a creation date for the plan.
[LIST NAMES]	List the names and affiliations of the planning committee members here, if applicable.

Goals and Realistic Strategies

Goals should have an audience and a benefit received by that audience because the library offers a specific service.

The realistic strategies to achieve goals (i.e., objectives) are composed of a time frame, a target, and a measure. Examples of measures are number of users, perceptions of users, outcomes, and units of service delivered, and can be both qualitative and quantitative.

Goals support the procurement of technology that ultimately benefits library patrons. See the template for examples. Please edit for your specific community needs.

Professional Development Strategy

Describe the level of staff development required over the next three years. Use the "Goal" and "Realistic Strategy" language described above.

Professional development opportunities support the staff's ability to deliver quality library services.

See the template for examples. Please edit for your specific community needs.

Assessment of Technology Resources

In this section of the technology plan, take an inventory of all the library's telecommunication services, hardware, software, and other services needed to improve library services. The inventory includes what the library currently has and what is required to meet standards. Whenever possible, the services and equipment should align with the library's goals and realistic strategies.

Using the form on page 159, enter the information as indicated. Use one form (or set of forms) for each year covered by the technology plan. Enter the year covered by the assessment in the top left corner of the form. Indicate in the table title whether you are class A, B, or C public library.

- Currently Have/Need. Enter the telecommunication service, hardware, software, and other service that the library currently possesses or offers. Also include items that the library needs to be in compliance with standards.
- Required by Standard. Review the public library standards (590 IAC 6) appropriate for the library's population class. Enter the standard on the form that corresponds with the entry in the "Currently Have/Need" column.
- Identified by Community Needs [compliance level will not be used]. List items identified to meet community needs for library technology services including hardware, software, and telecommunications.
- Compliance Level [Basic, Enhanced, Exceptional, Improve]. Place a mark in the box that indicates the library's level of compliance with the standard identified in the "Required by Standard" column. If the library is not in compliance, place a mark in the "Improve" box.

This section of the plan should be evaluated and updated annually.

Note: The detailed technology assessment on this form may be used in the long-range plan required by Indiana public library standards. Because a long-range plan can cover up to five years, additional years may need to be added to the assessment in the library's technology plan.

Equipment Replacement Schedule

Each year the library replaces or rotates equipment to best serve the needs of the library's community. This is illustrated in the library's equipment replacement schedule. Whenever possible, equipment replacement should align with the goals and realistic strategies of the technology plan.

Keep in mind that the library may already have an equipment replacement policy in place. The schedule in the technology plan should reflect such a policy.

The following rules of thumb may be used as guidelines for equipment replacement:

Notebook computers	3–4 years
Desktop computers	4–5 years
Servers	3–4 years
PDA/phones	2–3 years
Network equipment	3–5 years
Printers (as needed)	5+ years

Using the form on page 160, enter the information as indicated. Use one form (or set of forms) for each year covered by the technology plan.

- Assessed Resource. Use the hardware list from the assessment above to fill in this section of the form. Be as detailed as necessary to ensure all equipment is listed.
- [YEAR] [Q1, Q2, Q3, Q4]. Indicate the year of the technology plan. In the column for each quarter, place a mark when the equipment will be replaced. If the equipment listed will not be replaced that year, put "NA" in all four quarters.

Financial Resources

A plan for financial sustainability throughout the duration of the library's technology plan should be included in this section.

The financial estimates outlined in this section of the plan should also be evaluated regularly (at least annually) for progress toward the library's goals and realistic strategies.

Complete the form on page 161 by entering information as indicated. Use one form (or set of forms) for each year covered by the long-range plan. Enter the year covered by the assessment in the top left corner of the form.

- Currently Have/Need. Review the assessment form completed above. Enter the list of resources and services the library will be assessing in the corresponding section of the budgeting form: telecommunication service, hardware, software, or other service.

• Funds [Operating, LIRF, LCPF, Rainy Day, Gift, eRate, Fund #]. For each item listed in the "Currently Have/Need" column, enter an estimated dollar amount for the cost of the resource or service in that year of coverage. For "Fund #" columns, enter a fund name relevant to the library. Note that technology expenses may have funds unique to their purpose, such as eRate or the State Technology Grant.

Note: The technology section on this form may be used in the long-range plan required by Indiana public library standards. Because a long-range plan can cover up to five years, additional years may need to be added to the financial resources listed in the library's technology plan.

Evaluation

A method of evaluation for the entire technology plan of at least an annual basis should be described in this section.

Certain portions of the plan should be evaluated annually, such as the assessments and financial resources sections. The realistic strategies outlined in the technology plan should also be evaluated regularly (at least annually) for progress toward the library's goals. This includes the strategy described for professional development.

Differing evaluation methods per individual library are acceptable in this section. Choose one that works best for the plan developed by the library board.

The table below is a suggested form that can be used to evaluate the goals set forth in the goal/strategy parts of the plan.

Timeframe:	Complete no later than 06/30/2012	
Library goal:	Children will be engaged in dynamic and challenging learning opportunities delivered by way of technology.	
Library objective:	In six months the library will add a children's workstation with age-appropriate learning software.	
Category	Software	Hardware
Item	Includes 50+ installed for ages toddler to pre–K	Kids CyberNet Station – Early Learning System
Cost	$0	$2000
Purchase date	09/30/2011	09/30/2011

Use this example as a guide to draft and evaluate other goals and strategies in the plan.

The table below is a suggested form to evaluate or monitor the financial resources. This budget outlines the cost of technology services.

Fund	2013	2014	2015
Operating			
IT personnel & benefits	$75,000	$78,000	$80,000
Library computer supplies/annual maintenance/repairs	$8,000	$10,000	$12,000
Library ILS maintenance	$116,250	$85,000	$85,000
IT staff training	$10,000	$10,000	$10,000
Public service staff training	$2,000	$2,000	$2,000
Library data—telecommunications	$5,000	$6,000	$7,5000
	$216,250	$191,000	$196,500
Capital Projects Fund			
Network infrastructure and improvements	$125,000	$125,000	$200,000
PC retirements and additions	$285,000	$420,000	$250,000
Special technical projects	$50,000	$50,000	$50,000
	$460,000	$595,000	$500,000

Technology Bond Fund

Infrastructure improvements $100,000

Total	$776,250	$786,000	$696,500

The form can be modified to meet requirements of the evaluated item.

Automation Plan

Please provide information on current or future implementation of integrated library system (ILS) for cataloging and circulation of items, creation and maintenance of patron records, and public access of bibliographic records in the library or from a remote site.

Please include the following areas of planning, implementation, and maintenance in the automation plan.

A. Planning

    1. Library's needs, goals, and objectives
    2. Collection growth and current size
    3. Weeding schedule of collection management
    4. Number of titles with MARC records
    5. Operating costs related to the automation project
    6. Upgrade plans
    7. Timeline
    8. Budget

B. Implementation

    1. Retrospective conversion
    2. Hardware
    3. Software
    4. Training of staff and customers
    5. Site preparation

C. Maintenance

    1. Hardware support
    2. Software support
    3. Network support (if needed)

Note: If the automation project involves more than one library, the plan should at least include the following:

    1. Evaluation of the collections from each library

2. Arrangement for interlibrary loan procedures between entities
3. Interlocal agreement between the entities involved including a process of dissolution
4. Creation of policies and procedures for each library involved
5. Development of maintenance agreements

Automation Project Recommendations

In addition to the overall automation plan, specific parts of the plan should include the following:

Bibliographic Records

1. (AACR) "Anglo-American Cataloging Rules" should be the standard for

   - Access points
   - Descriptive cataloging
   - Original cataloging

2. Holdings information should also be kept current.

MARC Records (Machine-Readable)   This section covers the structure of the bibliographic records during conversion, import, and/or export.

1. The standard for the bibliographic records should be compliant with the most current MARC standard.
2. The bibliographic records should contain at least one of the following identifiers: LCCN (Library of Congress Control Number), ISBN (International Standard Book Number), or ISSN (International Standard Serial Number).
3. The standard for authority records should be the USMARC format for Authority Data, current edition.

Bibliographic Database

1. Database that is used as a local catalog should include all cataloged holdings unless otherwise noted.
2. The database should be maintained so that each bibliographic record accurately reflects the collection.
3. Additions and deletions to the collection and changes in the holdings and locations should be recorded within one month.
4. All records entered into the database shall follow the recommendations in the sections of bibliographic records and the MARC records.

Authority Control   It is recommended that either the Sear's Subject Headings or the Library of Congress Subject Headings be used as a resource.

Automation System (Software) Recommendations

- Should allow for database creation and maintenance and at a minimum either a circulation module or public access catalog module. It is recommended that libraries add additional modules as needed locally.
- Should have a backup system to protect and maintain the library's records.
- Should be able to import and export the current version of MARC records through at least one of the following ways: magnetic tape, floppy disk, or electronic file through the Internet.
- The library should create policies and procedures that relate to the operation of the system.

Automation System Hardware Recommendations

- The workstations and/or server should at minimum comply with the automation vendor's hardware and software recommendations. It is also suggested to surpass the minimum requirements given by the vendors.

References

ASCLA. 2010. "Assistive Technology: What You Need to Know Library Accessibility Tip Sheet 11." American Library Association. Accessed September 2017. http://www.ala.org.

Brown, C. D. 2016. *Crash Course in Technology Planning*. Santa Barbara, CA: Libraries Unlimited.

Burke, J. 2016. *Neal-Schuman Library Technology Companion: A Basic Guide for Library Staff*. Chicago: Neal-Schuman.

Dockery, Diana, interview by Diana Silveira. 2017. *Security of Small Technology* (November 15).

Gross, M., C. Mediavilla, and V. A. Walter. 2016. *Five Steps of Outcome-Based Planning and Evaluation for Public Libraries*. Chicago: ALA Editions.

Hernon, P., R. E. Dugan, and J. Matthews. 2014. *Getting Started with Evaluation*. Chicago: ALA Editions.

Krueger, R. A. 2002. "Designing and Conducting Focus Group Interviews." Eastern Illinois University, October 2002. Accessed April 4, 2018. http://www.eiu.edu.

KU Center for Community Health and Development. 2018. "Section 6: Conducting Focus Groups." Community Tool Box. Accessed April 5, 2018. https://ctb.ku.edu.

Mallery, M., ed. 2015. *Technology Disaster Response and Recovery Planning: A LITA Guide*. Chicago: American Library Association.

M-Lab. n.d. "M-Lab." Accessed June 27, 2017. https://www.measurementlab.net.

New York Public Library. n.d. "Other Assistive Technologies." New York Public Library. Accessed September 2017. https://www.nypl.org.

Schlipf, F. A., and J. A. Moorman. 2018. *The Practical Handbook of Library Architecture: Creating Building Spaces that Work*. Chicago: ALA Editions.

Stewart, A. W., C. Washington-Hoagland, and C. T. Zsulya, eds. 2013. *Staff Development: A Practical Guide*. Library Administration and Management Association. Chicago: American Library Association.

TechSoup. n.d. "Replacing and Upgrading Technology." TechSoup for Libraries. Accessed August 17, 2017. http://www.techsoupforlibraries.org.

U.S. General Services Administration. 2018. GSA Government-wide Section508 Accessibility Program. Section508.gov. Accessed September 2017. https://www.section508.gov.

World Wide Web Consortium (W3C). 2017. Home page. W3C. Accessed September 2017. https://www.w3.org.

Index

network security, 35, 61, 113–115
network servers, 5, 35
New America's Open Technology Institute, 3
New Horizons Report, 19
New York Public Library, 54
Niche Academy, 103
NonVisual Desktop Access (NVDA), 53

objectives, 70, 71, 78
obsolete technology, 33, 36–37
Oculus Rift, 16
office suites (software), 51
on-demand learning. *See* training
online forms. *See* forms
online learning. *See* training
openclipart.org, 31
OpenLDAP, 36
open-source software, 50–52
Open Web Application Security Project, 115
operating systems (computers), 37, 51
outcomes, 43–44, 69–70, 134
outsourcing. *See* consultants; maintenance (of technology), outsourcing of
Ozobots, 4, 8, 115, 117, 119, 127, 133

partnerships, 65, 75, 118
passwords, 17, 114, 123
patrons. *See* library users
PDF, 74
peripherals (computers), 3, 35, 54
personas, 21–22
personnel. *See* library staff
phishing. *See* cybersecurity
phones (mobile). *See* mobile devices
photo editing, 20, 21, 41, 51
Photoshop, 13
Piktochart, 138
PlanetLab (Princeton University), 3
planning, 55, 68–71; philosophy of, xii
planning committee, 29, 30, 69, 146
planning process, xii, xiii–xv, 29–30, 145, 149–151
podcast station, 40, 82, 97, 98, 105, 126
Pokemon GO, 16
PosterMyWall, 89
posters. *See* visual images
power outlets. *See* electrical service

press release, 91
Princeton University's PlanetLab, 3
printer, 3, 111, 117, 119, 121. *See also* 3-D printer
privacy, 16, 17–18, 51
PR Newswire, 91
programming, 16, 56
project management, 77–81
projectors, 4, 34
promotion. *See* marketing
protecting library technologies. *See* security (physical items)
public. *See* library users
public computers (workstations, computer labs), 18, 71, 115, 126
purchasing library technologies, 48, 50, 52, 56, 79, 120

RAM, 48, 116
ransomware. *See* cybersecurity
reboot to restore software. *See* Deep Freeze
reference department, 29
resume software, 12
robotics, 4
router, 3, 35, 55, 61, 111, 114

SaaS. *See* software as a service
Samsung Gear VR, 16
Screen Readers, 53. *See also* assistive technology
Section 508 Accessibility Program, 53
security (network). *See* cybersecurity
security (persons), 58
security (physical items), 33, 58, 115
security vulnerabilities (adware, malware and ransomware). *See* cybersecurity
senior citizens, 20–21, 96
serial number, 5
servers (computers), 3, 17, 37, 48–49, 103, 110, 111, 143–144
service-level agreements, 50, 121–122, 126
signage, 85, 88. *See also* visual images
Siri. *See* Apple, Siri
SketchUp, 17
Skype, 82, 99
Slack, 51
Small Business Administration, 65
small business community, 41–42, 96; creating space for services, 55, 58, 61;

Index

About the Author

Diana Silveira is president of Novare Library Services, a company that focuses on consulting with libraries with an emphasis on implementing and integrating new technologies. Her library experience includes serving as manager of virtual reference for Florida's Ask a-Librarian service; as coordinator of Florida's statewide delivery system for interlibrary loans; and as reference librarian at Charlotte Mecklenburg (NC) Library. Silveira is a regular presenter on such topics as implementing technology and applying best practices to maximize effectiveness in assisting users. She also consults with libraries that seek to develop new mobile and desktop websites or to deploy new technologies. She has a bachelor's degree in psychology from Catawba College and an MLIS from the University of North Carolina at Greensboro.